RUDOLF STEINER (1861–1925) called his spiritual philosophy 'anthroposophy', meaning 'wisdom of the human being'. As a highly developed seer, he based his work on direct knowledge and perception of spiritual dimensions. He initiated a modern and universal 'science of spirit', accessible to anyone willing to exercise clear and unprejudiced thinking.

From his spiritual investigations Steiner provided suggestions for the renewal of many activities, including education (both general and special), agriculture, medicine, economics, architecture, science, philosophy, religion and the arts. Today there are thousands of schools, clinics, farms and other organizations involved in practical work based on his principles. His many published works feature his research into the spiritual nature of the human being, the evolution of the world and humanity, and methods of personal development. Steiner wrote some 30 books and delivered over 6000 lectures across Europe. In 1924 he founded the General Anthroposophical Society, which today has branches throughout the world.

The Inner Nature of Man

and Our Life Between Death and a New Birth

*Eight lectures and a short address
given in Vienna from 6 to 14 April 1914*

Rudolf Steiner

Translated by A. R. Meuss

Rudolf Steiner Press

Rudolf Steiner Press
Hillside House, The Square
Forest Row, RH18 5ES

www.rudolfsteinerpress.com

First edition Rudolf Steiner Press 1994
Reprinted 2013

Originally published in German under the title *Inneres Wesen des Menschen und Leben zwischen Tod und neuer Geburt* (volume 153 in the *Rudolf Steiner Gesamtausgabe* or Collected Works) by Rudolf Steiner Verlag, Basel. This authorized translation is published by permission of the Rudolf Steiner Nachlassverwaltung, Dornach

Translation © Rudolf Steiner Press 2013

All rights reserved. No part of this publication may be reproduced, stored in a retrieval system, or transmitted, in any form or by any means, electronic, mechanical, photocopying or otherwise, without the prior permission of the publishers

A catalogue record for this book is available from the British Library

ISBN: 978 1 85584 378 3

Cover by Morgan Creative featuring 'Angel of Death' by Ninetta Sombart (reproduced with permission)
Typeset by PPS, Amesbury
Printed by Berforts Ltd., Herts.

Contents

Description of contents	v
LECTURE ONE *to the public, Vienna, 6 April 1914* The Quest for the Spirit in the Present Age	1
LECTURE TWO *to the public, Vienna, 8 April 1914* The Soul in the Light of Spiritual Science	30
LECTURE THREE *to members, Vienna, 9 April 1914* The Four Spheres of the Inner Life	59
LECTURE FOUR *to members, Vienna, 10 April 1914* The Vision of the Ideal Human Being	75
LECTURE FIVE *to members, Vienna 11 April 1914* The Senses and the Luciferic Temptation	89
LECTURE SIX *to members, Vienna, 12 April 1914* Wisdom in the Spiritual World	105
LECTURE SEVEN *to members, 13 April 1914* Between Death and the Cosmic 'Midnight Hour'	122
LECTURE EIGHT *to members, Vienna, 14 April 1914* Pleasures and Sufferings in the Life Beyond	138
SHORT ADDRESS *given before Lecture Eight* The St. John's Building, Dornach	154
Notes	157
Further Information	164

Description of Contents

Lecture One

Vienna, 6 April 1914
New insights into the physical world. The importance of strengthening attentiveness and devotion. Modern education is grounded in natural science; there is a growing longing for spiritual science. Kant and the limits of knowledge. Haeckel, Ostwald and materialistic thinking. Natural science has removed a perstitions. Cinema, passive people and the need for inner activity. The Old Testament, the Temptation and freedom. Those who oppose spiritual science are like those who opposed Copernicanism.

Lecture Two

Vienna, 7 April 1914
Spiritual research is to receive truths. Human beings must strengthen their dormant powers; spiritual exercises. The gate of death and the other side of memory. From memory to Imagination. Understanding the harmony between successive earth lives. Spiritual science reveals the soul's true nature. The panorama of life after death. Out-of-body experiences. Duration of after-death experiences varies according to life-span. Alternating periods of solitude and sociability. The path of incarnation. Criminals and their attitude to life. People who die early. Diseases and accidents. Copernicus, Giordano Bruno. Spiritual science is against present-day mainstream thinking. Goethe, Lorenzo de Medici.

Lecture Three

Vienna, 9 April 1914
Sensory perception, thinking, feeling and willing. The life between death and rebirth. Awareness of how we fall short of our potential. Leaving the body to contact someone who has died. With clairvoyant consciousness the world view is reversed. Seeing the human physical and ether bodies from outside. Destiny and its links with the body, the musculature and skeleton. *The Soul's Probation*. Man's being is born from the divine world. *Ex deo nascimur*.

Lecture Four

Vienna, 10 April 1914
Gaining spiritual perception through the soul element which is akin to memory. Imagination is similar to memory. Strengthening the power of recollection; this method places one in a different time. The realm between death and a new birth. The image of the ideal human being is the religion of the gods. It is beheld by human beings in the spiritual world. On earth we can lose sight of it. The path to the ideal. The temptation by Lucifer. The attraction of the parents for the soul. The physical body, a veil, shuts out the Luciferic temptation. Coming to know that we born out of God. *Ex deo nascimur*.

Lecture Five

Vienna, 11 April 1914
Sensory perceptions are a small part of what surges towards us; we are unaware of much. How the Guardian of the Threshold closes the door against Lucifer, who wants us to rise into the spiritual world. Spiritual beings live in our feelings. Much of our feelings and will are hidden from us by the Guardian. In ancient

times humans had more connection between their inner and outer life. Religious thinking is of things which will be active is us after death. The body, once transparent, is now coated like a mirror; we have ego consciousness. The evolution of thinking; the longing to awaken to new consciousness, which is restored by Christ, who lives in us. We send our dying elements down into Christ, and *In Christo morimur*.

Lecture Six

Vienna, 12 April 1914
After death, wisdom approaches the human being; the less we can absorb, the less we can develop powers to approach the ideal human being. Materialists after death are surrounded by wisdom, and can drown in the spirit. How telling lies and laziness on earth can torment after death. Spiritual science transforms our souls on earth, changes instincts and makes us more skilful. Karma and illness. On earth, we ask questions of things; in the spiritual worlds, things and realitities ask questions of human beings. Our inner being contains the answers. Old and new forms of clairvoyance. The need to develop and apply the will, and to prepare ourselves in the physical world. The idea of God by philosophers Lotze, Hegel and Soloviev. Finding the right relationship to Christ, and the way to enter the spirit. *In Christo morimur*.

Lecture Seven

Vienna, 13 April 1914
The time of passing through the gate of death. Seeing the earth and firmament from outside. Cosmic radiant wisdom. Life panorama passes in days and is transformed. Developing powers which were dormant on earth, and the transformation of memory. After death the human being is like an infant, with no self-awareness. The star of the will and the fruits of the past life. The

hankering for the body. Communication with the living, bonds of love. Feeling and will, separate in the life on earth, are united after death. The alternation of periods of solitude and sociability. The cosmic 'midnight hour'. The longing for positive creative power. The awakening to cosmic existence by the Holy Spirit: *Per spiritum sanctum reviviscimus.*

Lecture Eight

Vienna, 14 April 1914
After death human beings perceive life's pleasures differently, and have a choice to achieve something new for the world, or to bask in them. Pleasure involves a debt to the universe. Bodily pleasures cause pain to some entities in the world of spirit. Suffering on earth brings, after death, powers of will. Lies told on earth bring torments which must again be balanced on earth. Karmic compensation, diseases, early deaths, accidents, materialists after death. The need for lectures on spiritual science, even when few attend. Money markets and over-production, the dire consequences. Most people are born prematurely from the spirit; this will be compensated. Spiritual science needs to speak more of the Christ impulse. *The Portal of Initiation.* Human beings will one day see the ether form of Christ and be awakened by the Holy Spirit: *Per spiritum sanctum reviviscimus.*

Short Address

Vienna, 14 April 1914
The St. John's Building, Dornach, a centre and symbol. Greek temples were dwellings for gods, the Gothic cathedral a whole with the people within; the St. John's building is spiritually transparent.

LECTURE ONE

The Quest for the Spirit in the Present Age

Vienna, 6 April 1914

THOSE OF YOU WHO ATTACH SOME VALUE to the form of spiritual science presented in these two lectures will have to consider a strange paradox which has arisen in human evolution. It is that a spiritual stream or impulse may be entirely right for a particular age, if seen from a higher point of view, but will at the same time be sharply rejected by the people of that age, rejected in a way which is also entirely understandable.

At the dawn of the present age, the impulse to see the universe in a new way came through Copernicus. It was right for the age in so far as human evolution made it necessary for the impulse to arise exactly at that time.[1] Yet for a long time to come it was also to prove wrong for the age, for it was opposed by all the people who wanted to hold on to old ways of thinking and to prejudices which had persisted for hundreds and thousands of years. Anthroposophy, an approach to life based on spiritual science, seems right for the age to those who believe in it, but there are still many people today who do not see it in that light. I believe, however, that in these two lectures I shall be able to show that at a deeply subconscious level humanity is longing for anthroposophy today and lives in expectation of it.

In the first place, those who are engaged in this science of the spirit see it as a discipline in which the scientific work of recent centuries is genuinely taken forward into the future. It would be utterly wrong to think that it in any way opposes the great triumphs, tremendous advances and far-seeing truths which natural science[2] has provided. The intention is rather that it shall serve for the exploration of the world of the spirit, just as natural science has served and still does serve for the exploration of the physical world. We might call it the offspring of modern scientific thinking, even if there are many who are inclined to doubt this.

To give you an idea – not proof, but an idea intended to help understanding – let me say the following about the relationship between anthroposophy as a science of the spirit and the approach used in natural science. If we consider the tremendous advances made in scientific knowledge over the last three or four hundred years, we can say that on the one hand science has yielded immense insights within the wide horizon of human perception, and on the other hand the scientific way of thinking has found practical application in everyday life. Wherever we look in technology and commerce we see the practical application of scientific laws and discoveries. To get an idea of how anthroposophy relates to these scientific advances, let me first of all use an analogy. We may consider a farmer who tills his fields and gathers his harvest. Most of the fruits gathered in the fields enter into the sphere of human life, being used for food, and only a small part is left over. This is used as seed for new crops, and it is the only part of which we may say that the germinating power and the powers which generate life and matter, powers inherent in the sprouting grain, are allowed to take effect. Most of the harvest which has been brought in is not allowed to follow its own inherent laws of growth and progression but is taken into a side stream, we might say, to provide food for humanity.

This is more or less how anthroposophists see the scientific discoveries made in the recent centuries. These have for the most part been used, quite rightly, to gain insight into the outer physical world perceptible to the senses and have been of practical use to humanity. Some of the ideas which have arisen from study of the natural world in recent centuries may be 'left over' in human souls, however, and not used to understand anything to do with the physical world, build machines, or nurture industries. This remnant is brought to life and allowed to follow its natural destination and laws of development, like grain used for seed. If people really give their minds to the magnificent fruits which science has yielded and let this insight live in their souls, if they have the kind of feeling which makes them ask: 'How can the concepts and ideas developed in natural science be used to illuminate and understand the inner life? Can they help us to see where the powers lie that generate the inner life?' and if, in the light of all that has been achieved, we ask these questions not in a theoretical sense but out of the fullness of our inner life, something emerges which can become part of human civilization in an age when natural science has been cultivated in its own ground for a time.

There is another way in which this science of the spirit may be called the offspring of scientific thinking, even if the methods used to study the spirit have to be different from those used to study the physical world. If we want to have the same kind of properly organized, sound scientific basis for our study of the spirit as for the study of the physical world in natural science, the thinking used in natural science must be transformed to make it an effective tool for our purpose. Something will be said in these lectures of how this may be achieved. Anyone who is firmly grounded in natural science will be qualified to realize that spiritual insights cannot be gained with the methods used by scientists. Inspired minds have said, over and over again, that we have to realize that our powers of insight are limited if we base ourselves on the safe ground of modern science. Natural science and Kantianism, to mention just these two, have helped to create the belief that human powers of perception are limited, and that it is not possible to penetrate the regions where the source-spring is to be found with which the soul must feel connected, and where we are able to realize that other forces are also involved, and not only the forces which can be understood by scientists. Scientists of the spirit are in full agreement with natural scientists on this point. The powers of perception which have made natural science great and to which natural scientists must adhere, do not allow us to enter into the realm of the spirit.

Yet the human soul also has other powers of perception, which lie dormant within it. These cannot be used for the run-of-the-mill activities of ordinary science but they can be brought out from the underground depths of the human soul, and if this is done they will change human beings. They give us new powers of perception and understanding, allowing us to penetrate regions which are closed to natural science. Using a term which I do not particularly value, but which does help to clarify the matter, it may be called a kind of 'spiritual chemistry' which allows us to penetrate the spiritual realms of existence. This 'chemistry' is similar to ordinary chemistry in so far as both use unfailing logic and methodical thinking; in all other respects it is the chemistry of the inner life of man.

Let me use another analogy: When we look at water, this has specific properties. Chemists will tell us it contains hydrogen and oxygen. Hydrogen is a gas which will burn; it is quite different from water. Would anyone who does not know anything about chemistry be able to look at water and see that it contains hydrogen? Water is a liquid; it does not burn, but actually puts out fire. In short, can anyone tell it contains hydrogen by just looking at it? But chemists take hydrogen from water.

The water is analogous to ordinary human beings and the way in which they are perceived in ordinary science. They are a combination of physical matter, life, and an element of soul and spirit. In the light of the philosophy of modern science, ordinary scientists are perfectly right in saying that if one looks at human beings it is not possible to say that they have an element of soul and spirit in them. It is therefore perfectly understandable if the existence of this element is utterly denied in the light of this philosophy. We might, however, just as well deny the essential nature of hydrogen.

We will, of course, have to prove that it is possible to use our 'chemistry' of soul and spirit to show this element of soul and spirit as distinct from the living physical body. This can be done. And the message of anthroposophy is that there is such a 'chemistry' of soul and spirit, just as the message Copernicanism gave to a greatly surprised world was that the earth does not stand still but moves at tremendous speed around the sun, whilst the sun is standing still. The works of Copernicus and his followers were on the *Index Prohibitorum*[3] until the nineteenth century, and to some extent the insights gained through anthroposophy will long remain on the 'Index' of all the philosophies which for a long time to come will not be able to let go of centuries-old prejudices and habits of thought. And yet, anthroposophy has been able to enter into human hearts and souls and is not exactly alien to the needs of our time. We have a small piece of evidence to show that this is so – I do not mean to boast, but it is something worth mentioning as evidence that anthroposophy is right for our age, even if knowledge of this still lies hidden in people's souls. The fact is that we are now in a position to build an independent school of spiritual science on independent Swiss soil; thanks to the understanding shown by friends of this movement we can now see the new round building with its double cupola on the hills of Dornach, near Basle, which is intended to be a first outward sign of what this science of the spirit has to contribute to modern civilization. The building work is in progress, with the two cupolas already visible in outline above the base, and this enables us to speak of anthroposophy with increased hope and inner satisfaction, despite all opposition and lack of understanding in the world at large.

The 'spiritual chemistry' of which I have spoken cannot, of course, be achieved with external methods and techniques visible to the eye. It happens entirely in the human soul, and the work to be done is inner work, in soul and spirit. Such work will not leave the soul as it is in everyday life, but will transform it into a completely new instrument of perception. 'Spiritual chemistry' does not mean any kind of 'miracle' workings, nor anything based on superstition, but making inner efforts in soul and spirit, based on powers we actually have and use in everyday life, though perhaps they are only used as a sideline, as it were. These need to be tremendously enhanced; they have to grow infinitely stronger if we are to gain insight into the realm of the spirit.

One power which is used fairly casually in the whole of our inner life and needs to be tremendously enhanced is the power of attentiveness. What do we mean by attentiveness? Well, it means we do not let life flow past in whatever form it takes; instead we pull ourselves together inwardly and direct the eye of the spirit to one object or another. We select individual objects, place them in the mind's field of vision and concentrate our powers of soul on them. It is fair to say that in everyday life, too, our inner life, which needs activity, is only possible because we are able to develop such an interest, lifting individual events, facts and creatures out of the stream of life as it flows past.

This kind of attentiveness is entirely necessary in everyday life. We shall come to realize more and more, especially when people are taking even a little interest in anthroposophy, that anything to do with memory, as people call it, is basically simply a matter of paying attention. This will open up important aspects, particularly in education. It would be reasonable to say that the more effort is made to let the soul be actively interested – in the case of children and young people and also in later life – the more will the power of memory be strengthened. On the one hand this will have a positive effect on the objects to which we have given our attention, and on the other hand, the more we are able to practise this giving of attention the more will our memory grow in power and intensity.

There is something else as well. Everybody has heard of the sad mental condition which we may call 'discontinuity of consciousness'. There are people who cannot look back over the whole of their life and know: I myself have had this or that experience. They do not know what they have lived through. It can happen that they leave home, having lost the thread of continuity in their inner experience; they leave home for neither rhyme nor reason, walking about like lost souls, and it may be years before they find their own self again and are able to connect with the experiences of their ego. Such things would never end as tragically as they often do if it was known that this integrity of consciousness, maintaining full inner conscious awareness, depends on the regular development of active interest.

Active interest, attentiveness, is therefore something we need in everyday life. To be scientists of the spirit we have to take it as our basis and develop it to strengthen the inner life, deepening it in what we may call 'meditation' and 'concentration'. These are the technical terms for the process. In ordinary life, life itself makes us turn our attention to one thing or another. Scientists of the spirit methodically direct the full powers of soul to an idea, an image, an inner response, will impulse or particular mood – which are clearly definable and apparent to the soul – and concentrate all their inner powers on them. The method involves suppressing all sensory activity directed at things outside, which normally happens only when we are in deep sleep. You must subdue all your thinking, all quest for goals, all cares and concerns of life, just as they are subdued in deep sleep. As far as ordinary life is concerned, therefore, you are then exactly as you are in deep sleep, except that you do not lose consciousness but remain fully awake. All the powers of soul which are normally scattered over outer experiences and the cares and troubles of life are concentrated on a single, deliberately chosen idea, inner response or the like, which is made the focus of your inner life. With the powers of soul thus concentrated, a faculty which generally lies dormant and only acts between the lines of your present life, as it were, emerges strongly from the human soul. It then actually happens that with attentiveness increased to an immeasurable degree and become highly concentrated and active, the soul learns to experience itself in itself in such a way as to be able to tear itself away from the physical body whilst fully conscious, just as hydrogen is removed from water by chemical methods.

It does, of course, take years of inner work to achieve the active attention and concentration needed to enable the spiritual investigator to tear himself away from the physical body. But the time will come when words which sound utterly peculiar to present-day people begin to have meaning for the spiritual investigator. These seemingly fantastic words are: 'I experience myself as soul and spirit outside the living physical body and I know that this body is outside the soul – well, just as this table is outside my body. I know that when the soul has grown strong it can have the experience of the body being there before it like a foreign object – this body and all the destinies it has to go through in ordinary life.' You, as you normally are, come to be completely outside when you experience yourself as soul and spirit separate from the body, and this soul and spirit entity then has completely different qualities from those it has when it is bound up with the physical body and its senses and uses the brain-bound intellect.

The first thing to happen is that the power of thought separates from physical experience. I do not want to talk in abstract terms, but give you real facts. Please do not take it amiss if I use plain words, without prejudice, to speak of things which still sound extremely odd today. When a spiritual investigator begins to find meaning in the words: 'You are now living in the soul; you know that your soul is a real non-physical entity in which you find yourself when you are outside your senses and brain,' he first of all feels as if his thinking is now outside the brain, alive and active all around the head. Between birth and death we must, of course, always return to the body, and spiritual investigators are able to observe the exact moment when they return to brain-bound thinking after a time when they have been purely in soul and spirit. They find that the brain offers resistance; they feel they come in on the waves of an earlier life which was purely in the spirit and slip into the physical brain,[4] which is then active in its usual way, following anything achieved in soul and spirit. To experience yourself out of the body and then entering into the body again is one of the most heart-moving experiences for the spiritual investigator.

Thinking which experiences itself purely in itself and takes place outside the brain is different from ordinary thinking. Our ordinary thoughts are like shadows compared with the thoughts which open up like a new world to spiritual investigators when they are out of the body. These thoughts are full of inner images, which is also why we call them 'Imaginations', not because we think them to be mere fantasy, something thought up, but because everything we experience in that condition is truly experienced in images. This kind of Imagination means you are really entering into things, with everything you come upon in the world of the spirit presenting itself to the mind's eye in images.

In this way thinking can be separated from the living human body, and spiritual investigators thus find themselves in a world of spiritual entities and events.

It is also possible to separate other human powers from the living physical body. When thinking is separated, spiritual investigators first of all experience themselves in their true essential nature as soul and spirit. Perception is, however, entirely different from our ordinary sensory perception, where the objects we perceive are outside us and we come face to face with them. When we are able to perceive with faculties which are free of the body, the spiritual world opens up around us with the same inevitability as colours and light arise for someone who was born blind and has been given sight through an operation. The experience is that you do not simply come face to face with things and entities in the world of the spirit, but actually enter right into them with your whole being. You then know that you perceive by flowing out into things and entities and becoming aware of them in the images they create for you to behold. You feel yourself to be in constant activity, and one way of describing the way you come to life in the world of imaginative thoughts would be as a spiritual kind of changing facial expressions. You tear your soul and spirit away from the living body, and this element of soul and spirit is in constant activity, entering into events in the world of the spirit and imitating the powers which are alive and active in them. Your connection with the spiritual entities is such that we may compare it with being face to face with someone and able to enter into their inner life to such an extent that your own face expresses the joy felt by the other individual. You enter with soul and spirit into the experiences of others and become the expression of those experiences. The essence of things comes to expression in your own spiritual character. You are driven to perceive actively. It is therefore reasonable to say that spiritual research makes completely different demands on the human soul from those made in ordinary research, where you are passive as you take note of things. It demands that the soul must be inwardly active and alive; it must be able to enter into things and entities and itself bring to expression what they present to it.

Thus it is possible to use 'spiritual chemistry' to isolate soul and spirit from the living body. It is also possible to do this with another power, one that is normally only used in the body and which may be said to pour into the body. Strange as it may sound, this is the power of speech.

When we speak, the situation is as follows. Our thoughts live in us; the brain, which vibrates with our thoughts, has a link with the organs of speech. Muscles are set in motion and our inner experiences flow out into words and live in our words. We can, and indeed from the point of view of anthroposophy must, say that when we speak we pour the things that live in the soul into the organs of the physical body. The power of speech can be isolated from the physical body with its senses, by increasing our power of attentiveness, as already described, and adding something more, which is that we increase, again beyond all limits, another faculty we possess, which is the power of devotion.

We feel this when we are in a religious mood, when we give our loving devotion to someone or something, dedicate ourselves to strict scientific discipline in the study of objects and laws, and when we are able to leave aside all thought and feeling related to the self. In everyday life, devotion really only runs between the lines. Spiritual investigators have to increase and strengthen it beyond all limits. They must be able to give themselves to the ongoing stream of existence in the way we are generally only given up to it – without in any way contributing to the experience – during deep sleep, when all movement of the limbs ceases, all senses are silent and we are giving ourselves up entirely, doing nothing ourselves. During sleep we are, of course, unconscious. We can, however, resolve to make it an inner exercise that is repeated over and over again to suppress all sensory activity, all movement of our limbs, and take life in the physical body with its senses into the state where it normally only finds itself in deep sleep. We can resolve to stay awake in the process, maintaining the full light of consciousness and developing the inner feeling of being poured into the ongoing stream of existence, and wanting nothing but what the world wants to do with us. If we can enter into this feeling over and over again, and do so quite separately from the faculty of attentiveness, the soul itself will grow stronger and stronger.

It is important to keep the two exercises – attentiveness and devotion – entirely separate, for they conflict. Attentiveness calls for maximum effort and concentration focused on a single object; it is deepened meditation. Devotion calls for giving ourselves passively to the ongoing stream of existence, increasing beyond limits the feeling we know in religious experiences and in loving devotion to someone else. The fruit of such a limitless increase in devotion and attentiveness is the ability to isolate the inner life of the soul from the living physical body. The power which is otherwise poured out into words, a power which acts by not existing in itself and for itself but setting the nerves in motion, can be isolated from thus coming to expression in speech, and remain in itself in the sphere of soul and spirit. The power of speech is then torn away from its physical and sense-bound context and we experience what Goethe called 'spiritual hearing'.[5]

Once again we find ourselves out of the body, but this time we enter into things and perceive their inner nature; we perceive them in such a way as to re-create them within us, as if with an inner gesture – not merely a facial expression, but an inner gesture. The activity of the soul and spirit element which has been torn away from the body is similar to what we do when we are tempted to use a special gift of imitation and express something we have in mind in a gesture. There we merely use a special gift; now the soul torn from the body does the same thing in order to perceive. It enters into things and actively re-creates the powers it perceives at work in them. In the world of the spirit, to perceive always means to be active; we perceive the things we enter into by re-creating the inner life and activity we find there. In the physical world we are passive when we listen and hear.

In our spiritual hearing, speech and hearing seem to become one. We enter into the essential nature of things and hear what lives in them. Pythagoras's 'music of the spheres' can be heard by the spiritual investigator. We enter into the objects and entities in the world of the spirit, and hear by giving utterance. It is the experience of speaking as you hear and hearing as you speak when you enter into the nature of things. This is true Inspiration.

A third inner activity and experience may come to spiritual investigators if they continue to develop enhanced attentiveness and devotion when out of the body. Let me present this in the following way.

Look at a child. (Time will not permit me to go into detail and I shall limit myself to brief mention of what matters to us today.) One of the characteristics of developing human beings is that they must find their own orientation in space during childhood. At birth they are unable to walk or stand, and to begin with they have to move on all fours. They then develop the inner powers which we may call 'powers of coming upright', and this leads to something, the significance of which has been felt by many deep thinkers who have said that, by being able to come upright into the vertical, human beings are able to look out into the far distances of cosmic space and their field of vision is not limited to the earth world. The most important thing, however, is that human beings have inner powers and are able to gain in strength and inner experience, thus developing from life in the horizontal, where they are helpless, to life in the vertical, standing upright. Natural scientists will simply have to realize that this inner human activity is very different from the hereditary powers which give animals their orientation in the world. The powers which give animals a particular orientation relative to the vertical, act in an entirely different way from the sum of powers[6] which tear human beings away from their position of helplessness. This sum of powers – it is a whole system, a large sum of powers – is inwardly active and gives human beings the orientation in space which makes them earthly human beings in the true sense of the word. The activities of these powers are deeply hidden, and we must have studied a certain amount of spiritual science before we are able to find them. Not all these powers are used up when we learn to walk and talk in childhood; some still lie dormant in us, but no use is made of them in our ordinary life in the sphere of the senses and in conventional science.

Doing the exercises in enhanced attentiveness and devotion, we become inwardly aware that the powers which made us come upright in childhood are still within us. We grow aware of non-physical powers of orientation and of movement, and the result is that, in addition to the inner faculties of giving facial expression and creating gesture, we develop an inner physiognomy of soul and spirit. When the soul and spirit are out of the living body, and spiritual investigators begin to know the meaning of the words: 'You now live in the soul and spirit',[7] the time also comes when they are aware of the powers which made them come upright as physical beings with physical senses on earth. They are then able to use these powers in a new way, giving them a new and different orientation, to take on a new and different form from the human form they had as children. They are now able to develop inner movements, adapt to any orientation in space, and give physiognomies to their spiritual element which differ from the physiognomy it has in the earth-bound human being. They are able to enter wholly into other spiritual events and beings, relating to them in such a way that the powers which transform the crawling infant into an upright human being are transformed inside the objects and entities of the spiritual world; they can assume their features and perceive these features by thus bringing them to expression. This is true Intuition.

Spiritual entities and events are truly perceived by entering into them and assuming their physiognomy. We experience anything which is alive and active in spiritual entities by giving inner facial expression to it. We live in their mobility by recreating their gestures. We assume their actual form by transforming ourselves into them, perceiving them by turning into them.

I did not want to use the terms generally used in philosophy to describe the method spiritual investigators use to enter into the world of the spirit in a living way. My intention was to give you a concrete picture, as far as possible, of how the living experience of soul and spirit tears itself away from perception based on the physical senses and enters wholly into the world of the spirit, where perception is based on inner activity. Every step taken into the world of the spirit must involve such inner activity, and we must always know that the things of that world do not offer their essential nature to us, and we can only know about things and events there if we are able to re-create them in active perception. The great difference between perception in the spirit and our ordinary perception in the physical world is that whilst ordinary perception is passive in giving itself up to things, spiritual perception means living in constant activity, so that we actually come to be whatever it is we wish to perceive.

People are still prepared – or, perhaps, again prepared – to forgive us if we speak in general terms of a world of the spirit. But it still sounds very strange in their ears when someone says: 'Human beings can leave behind all sensory perception such as seeing and hearing, and also all thinking that is bound to the nerves and the brain. Then, when everything we experience in and around us in physical life has vanished, we can know ourselves to be in a completely new, real world where the entities and events are purely spiritual, just as entities and events are physical here in the physical world.'

What anthroposophy has to offer is no nebulous pantheism, no hodgepodge kind of life in mind and spirit. Compared with anthroposophy, to speak of pantheism is rather like saying: 'I am taking you into a meadow where plants are growing; this is nature, pan-nature' and then taking people into a laboratory and saying: 'This is nature, pan-nature. All the flowers and the creeping things, the trees and shrubs, all the chemical and physical processes are pan-nature!' People would be far from satisfied with such a way of presenting nature in the round, for they know very well that the only way they can manage to understand is by considering individual aspects. Rather than a hodgepodge kind of life in mind and spirit, anthroposophy offers real, concrete events and entities which can be perceived in the world of the spirit. Anthroposophists must not be afraid of challenging the people of their age, but say: Here in the physical world we see physical people around us who come first in the 'hierarchy' of minerals, plants, animals and humans, but all this vanishes beyond the horizon of the mind when we come alive in the world of the spirit; spiritual realms and hierarchies will then emerge, entities which are equal to human beings and others which are higher up in the hierarchy. On earth, we have animals, plants and minerals below human beings in the hierarchy; in the other world, entities and creatures exist at levels above the human level in higher spheres of being – individual spiritual entities and creatures.

In the second lecture we shall speak of how the human soul has its place in the world of the spirit, and of the life it lives in that world. This is based on the science of the spirit of which an outline has been given today. We shall also consider the path the human soul has to follow when it has gone through the gate of death and entered a world of pure spirit. The lecture will give various insights into life after death which have been gained through the science of the spirit.

The method developed in anthroposophy as a science of the spirit is obviously very different from anything people find acceptable, for they live with habits of thought which have evolved through the centuries and are as firmly established as habits of thought people had at the time when Copernicus presented his system of the universe. The question we must face is how the science of the spirit should relate to the quest of the age, if it is to see itself in the right light and have the right attitude to this quest of the age.

The first objection, one frequently raised at the present time, is that spiritual scientists speak of developing special powers of soul to enable us to see into the world of the spirit. They feel there is nothing in all this for people who have not developed such powers and are not able to create spiritual images and separate their thinking, powers of speech and orientation in space from the body. That, of course, is like saying that paintings have nothing to offer to anyone who cannot paint – which would be a sad thing – and that you must have learned how to paint in order to appreciate a picture. But it would be a very sad thing if pictures only meant something to the people who are able to paint them. The fact is that when we see a picture, we have natural powers which enable us to understand it even if we are not able to paint. The human soul has a language which allows it to relate to all art that is alive. And the same holds true in the case of anthroposophy. You have to be a scientist in this field to discover and describe the facts, events and entities of the world of the spirit. However, when such a scientist takes care to clothe the things of that world in ordinary thoughts and ideas, and express them in words – which is what I have attempted to do today – anyone can understand them, even without being a scientist. All you have to be able to do is to clear from your mind anything connected with modern education, which presents itself as being firmly grounded in natural science but which, in truth, is not grounded in it but merely believes itself to be so. If you let go of all bias and look without prejudice at the picture presented by the spiritual scientist, the fruits of spiritual science are accessible to everyone. Human souls are made for the truth and they are sensitive to it; they are not made for untruth and inaccuracies. All it needs is to clear away the debris which has collected because of prejudice. Deep down in the human soul is a secret, intimate language which enables people of all backgrounds, educational and otherwise, to understand the spiritual scientist, if they are willing.

This is exactly what scientists of the spirit see when they consider the quest of our age. In earlier centuries people were convinced that the only way of knowing anything about the world of the spirit was to believe. In more recent times they have been able to think that certain knowledge must always be based on external facts. Today the situation is that whilst people in general may not yet know it in the upper layers of consciousness – that is, in clear concepts, ideas and feelings – scientists of the spirit know quite clearly: 'We live in an age when a longing for the science of the spirit is developing deep down in human souls; it is their true hope.' People will come to realize more and more that old prejudices must go, especially in our ways of thinking.

Today many people – particularly people who feel they are on solid philosophical ground – are still saying: 'Surely Kant has shown, and physiology[8] has shown, that we can know nothing of what lies behind the world we perceive with the senses. And now these scientists of the spirit want to go against Kant and show that this fact, so clearly established in modern physiology, is wrong.' Spiritual science has no intention of showing that the statements made by Kant and modern physiologists from their point of view are wrong. Yet the people of our age, and those involved in the quest, which is still below the surface in our age, will find that there is a point of view other than calling things right or wrong. Let us see how practical experience in real life looks in relation to this, for it is the most fruitful kind of experience.

It would be possible for someone to provide strict proof of the fact that human beings are unable to see cells, for example, with the naked eye. This person might be entirely correct, just as it would be correct to say that with the human faculties known to Kant it is not possible to enter into the essential nature of things. Let us assume the microscope has not been invented, and it has been proved that people cannot see the smallest particles. This would be correct. The proof would really work in every respect, and there could be no objection to the strict proof that the human eye cannot see the smallest partial organisms which make up large organisms. The issue became immaterial, however, with the advance of science; what mattered was that, irrespective of the proven facts, physical instruments could be developed – the microscope, the telescope and all the rest – in order to achieve what demonstrably could not be achieved when human faculties were used unaided. People are right when they say human faculties are limited. Spiritual science does not contradict them; it merely shows that human powers of perception can be enhanced and strengthened in the spirit, just as it is possible to increase our physical powers. It may be absolutely right to hold the opposite view, but spiritual science must be beyond this kind of right and wrong. One day people will no longer insist on everything being proved with the limited powers of proof at our disposal. They will realize that life demands quite different things from human evolution than the logical certainties on which people like to depend.

Something else has to be said if the true – and not just the imagined – quest of our age is to be seen in connection with the true goal and purpose of spiritual science. Let me again refer to the truly enormous advances made in natural science. In the light of these it is not surprising that people think they can build a whole world on the solid ground of modern science, though this does not take account of the powers of which we have spoken today. Materialistic thinking is already widespread today; it calls itself by the somewhat more elegant name 'monism', because 'materialistic' does not sound so good. The head of this monistic stream is Ernst Haeckel, a man of considerable reputation in his field of natural science,[9] and its lieutenant-general is Wilhelm Ostwald.[10] With monism, the idea is to create a philosophy by developing the insights which can be gained from natural science only. People who take up the quest of our age will come to realize that natural science is on solid ground for as long as it limits itself to studying the laws and principles of the physical world. And it has achieved great things. One of its great achievements is that it has swept away old prejudices. Faust still used an outer, physical form of magic in his dealings with the natural world; anyone who understands modern science can no longer use such magic. It is quite another thing that the life of the spirit itself creates an inner magic of the soul by the means I have described.

Modern science has done great things in overcoming superstition and doing away with methods of explaining the natural world in the way one would 'explain' a watch by saying: 'There are hobgoblins in there'; it has done great things in overcoming a way of looking at nature which wants to have all kinds of ghosts behind the phenomena of the physical world. Its great achievements have been in negation, also as a philosophy. Take a good look at 'scientific naturalism' and how it functions when it is a matter of getting rid of old, unhealthy notions of all kinds of invented fantasy figures behind the world of nature. For as long as this kind of thinking exists and has to be opposed, natural philosophy finds a reason for existence in fighting the things which have to be fought.

In a sense, however, this fight has had its day; it has done the good it can do. Today the quest of our age is to ask: 'What means can we use to build an image of the world which has room for the human soul?' And this is where natural philosophy and Haeckel's and Ostwald's materialism fail us completely, if human beings perceive themselves to be what they really are. Those who take up the quest of our age will come to understand more and more clearly that the people who hold purely materialistic views make excellent soldiers to fight old superstitions. Now, however, they are old warriors who have done their duty but lack the ability to develop the arts of peace, develop industries and till the fields. It cannot be denied that natural science is outstanding as a philosophy when it is a matter of fighting superstition. For as long as the people who make it their philosophy can go on fighting, this fight means something to their souls and keeps them going. Yet when they then want to create a real image of the world in which there is room for the human soul, they are like old warriors who have no talent for the arts of peace. They then have to face the question in their souls in peacetime, as it were, and they do not arrive at an image of the world.

A mood like this will grow in human souls as time goes on;

the spiritual investigator is already able to perceive such moods in the depths of those souls. They may not yet be aware of it, but people are longing for the fruits of spiritual science. This is the secret of the present age. From a higher point of view, therefore, spiritual science is entirely right for our age, yet for many people, who are not yet able to look deep down and perceive what it is they really want, it is wrong for our age. It therefore seems to them that the image of the world presented in spiritual science has no solid scientific foundation. The image of the world presented by monism is thought to be firmly based on the science of the physical world. Looking at the opposite side of the coin we may see what must happen if the soul truly wants to see its hopes and longings fulfilled. The activity demanded in spiritual science gives something to the soul which really lifts it up to communion in the spirit, so that we are able to use active perception and gain insight into the spiritual world in its activity. Spiritual science enables us to know the reality of the true world of the spirit. Monism has nothing to say about this for the people who take up the quest of our age.

The quest of our age, the search in which human souls are engaged, cannot be suppressed, however. The result is that some people have got into the habit of directing their inner thoughts [relating to things of the spirit] in such a way that their thinking is like that of natural science – looking passively at the world outside them. Basically the situation is that some people – anyone who has been considering this will know about it – want to look at the things of the spirit in the way one looks at the physical world. I am not saying this will not lead to the truth in some cases; but the method is different from the one used in spiritual science. Spiritualism, or spiritism, is a school of thought where people want to see spiritual entities and events by looking at them passively from outside, in the way we look at events in the physical world; they do not wish to become inwardly active in perception and rise into the worlds of the spirit. Where does this spiritism, which may fairly be said to be materialistic, spring from? It springs from the philosophical approach represented by 'monism' and holds to the superstition of materialism, to the belief that everything is governed by laws of nature. Some will say they find it hard to believe that spiritism is actually supposed to be the child of Haeckel's monism. People who follow the quest of our age will find that much the same thing happens with this child as with all offspring. Fathers and mothers often have marvellous ideas as to what their child will be like and yet as often as not the child will turn into a real brat. What matters is not the civilized child that is the dream of monism, but what the child actually turns out to be. Utter belief in the material world will generate the belief that the spirits, too, can only act in material ways and reveal themselves in material form. If purely monistic materialism were to grow, spiritist associations and spiritist views would grow and flourish to the same degree, creating the necessary counter-image. The more the people who blindly follow the way shown by Haeckel and Ostwald manage to suppress a true science of the spirit, the more will they find that they are breeding spiritism, which is the other side of the coin when it comes to a true science of the spirit. Spiritual scientists who are firmly based on a life of the spirit[11] which can be explored, perceived and known, will be quite unable to follow a method where one seeks to materialize the spirit and give oneself up to it passively, for the spirit can only be known through inner activity.

I am now going to consider another aspect of this quest of our age, which is as yet unable to understand itself inwardly. A philosopher who deserves our esteem has published a strange essay in a widely read journal.[12] Among other things, he says that many people find Spinoza and Kant quite difficult to read. They get easier as you go on, but their concepts are always shifting and changing. Well, it cannot be denied that this holds true for many people. The author of the essay gives some advice, however, on how it may be done differently and in accord with the quest of our age. According to him, technology now provides us with the means of getting a good picture of the confusing, abstract ideas presented by Kant and Spinoza. He wants to use a kind of cinematography to show Spinoza sitting and grinding glass as the idea of extension comes to him. This is to be shown in a sequence of changing images. The image of extension will then be transformed into the image of thinking, and so on. Cinematography could thus be used to create a visual image of Spinoza's whole ethics and philosophy, and this would satisfy those who follow the quest of our age. Oddly enough, the editor of the journal even commented that an invention which may seem no more than a toy to some people could therefore meet an ancient human need in a way which is entirely in accord with our age.

Now it may be possible, in some respects, to satisfy the questing minds of our time, though only with regard to outer things, by presenting Spinoza's *Ethics* or Kant's *Critique of Pure Reason* cinematographically. Why not? It would be in line with the passive attitude so popular today. It is so popular that people find it hard to believe that the reality [of the things of the spirit] can only be found by going through everything yourself. Our age does not yet accept an approach where you bring the essential nature of these things to expression in your own inner life. Imagine you are standing by a notice board and trying to read the minds of the people who are looking at it. An advertised lecture where no slides are shown and the audience are expected to share in the effort of generating the thoughts presented by the speaker will have a smaller audience than one where it says slides will be shown to illustrate the subject, which means that people will be allowed to be entirely passive.

Anyone who looks more deeply into the quest of our age and to its deepest, as yet unconscious, longings and hopes, will find that the impulse to be active, to find oneself again as a soul in full inner activity, is to be found deep down in human souls. Our inner life can only be independent and have moral security if we are inwardly active. It can only have a proper orientation in life if we become aware that we are more than the things we receive passively from the world, for we are also involved in anything we are able to experience through being active. When it comes to the world of the spirit, human souls can only gain insight into whatever they are able to make their own by being active. If we think the things through which we are given in spiritual science, the effort to grasp them makes us share in the activity, and that is why spiritual science can satisfy the deepest, subconscious impulses in human souls today and help the quest of our age that lies deep down in human souls.

We are in a period of transition where these things are concerned. It is of course easy to say such commonplace words as 'we are in a period of transition'. All times are times of transition. If we do speak of a period of transition, it is important to say in which respect we are in transition. To describe the transition occurring in our age we have to say that it has been necessary for humanity to undergo training in passivity, for this was the only way in which the sciences, with everything that has made them great, could achieve their great advances. It was necessary for people to give themselves entirely to the truths of the material world, so that what had to be achieved could be achieved, especially in the sciences. Life, however, goes in rhythms. Just as a pendulum swings one way and then the other, so the human soul, having been rightly trained in faithful passive devotion, must gather itself up again and become active, in order to find itself in itself. As to what has become of the soul because of its passivity – I am now going to use words that will sound utterly radical, but I will not fight shy of saying them, even if they sound extremely odd to many people. On the other hand it is exactly when you enter fully into spiritual science that you realize that not to make such a radical statement actually means you are not prepared to face the consequences of the natural-scientific approach. It means you do not have the courage to draw the inevitable conclusions; the people who insist they base themselves wholly and entirely on the findings of natural science also do not have the courage. If we were consistent in this, we would hear a murmur of strange words going through the quest of our age.

At the beginning of the Old Testament we have the words – I shall not go into their inner meaning today; people may take these words in whichever way they can; some may take them to present an image, others for fact, but everyone will agree with what I have to say about them today – 'And you will be like God himself, knowing – or distinguishing – both good and evil.' These are the words which have come down to us with the Old Testament, and whichever way you take them, you will have to admit they hold great significance for human nature and the human soul. The story tells of the tempter approaching the human being and murmuring in his ear: 'If you follow me you will be like a god, able to tell the difference between good and evil.'[13] You can sense that the inclination towards things other than good would not have arisen in human beings if it had not been for this temptation; without it, humanity would be inclined only towards the good. The whole of human freedom therefore has to do with what is said in these words. It is said that human beings were invited by the tempter to go beyond themselves and see themselves as something they are not – to be like a god with regard to good and evil. As I said, you may think about this in any way you like and I really do not ask anyone to take the tempter to be a real entity, though for anyone who is able to see through these things it is quite true that 'They never dream the devil is about, not even if he has them by the collar.'[14] Anyone who is even a little bit able to listen to the quest of our age will hear his murmurings again, for he is approaching. Call it the inner voice or whatever – we can say that he is here, and this is no superstition. For people who have the courage to draw the final conclusion of a philosophy of life based entirely on natural science, he has highly characteristic things to say – a strange wisdom. The problem is that the people who claim to base themselves entirely on natural science do not have the courage to draw the final conclusion. In their hearts and minds they still believe in good and evil, though they ought to deny the existence of such things when basing themselves purely on natural science. As soon as we base ourselves purely on natural science it surely is true that not only does the sun shine on good and evil alike, but the laws of nature are such that our human nature makes us do evil just as much as good. The tempter has drawn this final conclusion and murmurs in human ears: 'Do you not see, you're simply more highly developed animals. You are like the animals and cannot tell good from evil.' Our time is a period of transition in so far as the tempter now says the opposite of what we are told he said in the Old Testament. He says: 'You are only more highly developed animals, and if you see yourselves as you really are, you cannot say there is a difference between good and evil.'

If people had the courage to draw this conclusion it would be the outcome of a philosophy which is entirely passive. It is the aim and purpose of anthroposophy to save our age from this voice – speaking metaphorically – and bring knowledge of life in the spirit into the quest of our age. People who continue to oppose this science of the spirit in the light of some other science will have to realize that their opposition is like the original opposition to Copernicanism. Now that we are building our own independent School of Spiritual Science we have come to the attention of a world which did not take much notice of us before, with the result that opposition is increasing. In a recent article[15] I pointed out how today's opponents of spiritual science are taking the same attitude as those who opposed Copernicus. Someone who felt, quite rightly, that this was directed at him, said in reply that Copernicus presented facts, whilst spiritual science was merely making assertions. The poor man did not realize that at one time the facts presented by Copernicus also were mere assertions and empty of meaning for people like him; he fails to appreciate that what he calls mere assertions are facts in the light of a true science, though of course they are facts relating to the life of the spirit. Both scientists and religious people are therefore raising objections to this science of the spirit. In Copernicus's day, people said: 'We cannot believe that the earth moves around the sun, for the Bible does not say so.' Today people say: 'We cannot believe what spiritual science tells us, for the Bible does not say so.' Nevertheless, people will come to accept what spiritual science has to say, just has they have come to accept what Copernicus had to say.

It is important always to remember the words of a profoundly learned man who was also a priest.[16] He taught at Basle University and in his inaugural lecture as vice-chancellor, which was on Galileo, said the beautiful words: 'In those days people opposed Galileo because they believed he was upsetting the tenets of religion; today anyone who is truly religious knows that every new truth discovered adds something to the original revelation of divine guidance and the glory and majesty of the divine plan.'

It would be good to draw the attention of our opponents to something which might well have been, though it did not actually happen. Imagine someone had gone to Columbus and said: 'We cannot allow you to discover the new continent' – which he then did discover – 'for life is fine as it is in the old world, with the sun shining on it all. How do we know the sun will also shine on any new countries which may be discovered?' This is how the spiritual scientist sees his religious ideas opposed by people who feel that the discoveries of spiritual science threaten their religious ideas. It must be a feeble faith, a religion built on shaky ground, if people think the sun of their religious feeling will not also shine in any new territory which is discovered in the realm of the spirit, just as the sun which shines in the old world also shines in the new world. People who consider the facts in an unbiased way can convince themselves of the truth of this. If in its quest our age can come to accept spiritual science more and more, it will be touched by it in a way undreamt of by many.

Spiritual science still has many opponents, which is understandable. It does, however, make us feel kinship with all the people who, even if they have not yet found spiritual science, do have an inkling of the soul's connection with the realms of the spirit to which spiritual science gives access. With regard to what has been said about the words which the tempter is murmuring today, we feel in harmony, for instance, with Schiller, who did have an inkling of those realms. Schiller did his own research in natural science and gained the impression that man must be seen as above mere animal existence and that the human soul has a share in the realm of the spirit. Taking our stand on spiritual science, we feel in deep accord with one of the leading lights in the philosophy of life which has been evolving in recent times, when we are able to epitomize what has been presented on a broader scale today in the feeling that was put in a nutshell in Schiller's words:

> Down came the barrier of animalic dumbness
> And human nature shone from brow thus clear'd.
> Thought now came, a noble stranger,
> Sprung from brain surprised.[17]

Spiritual science confirms that animal nature has been left behind and human beings now belong to a realm of spirit; this is how it stands with regard to the quest of our age.[18]

Finally, let me remind you of someone who lived and worked here in Austria and whose soul, with great inwardness, dimly felt what has now become certainty in spiritual science. He stood all alone in his thinking and vision, holding fast to a spiritual point of view despite the fact that as a physician he could base himself fully on natural science. Let us take the words of Baron Ernst von Feuchtersleben,[19] for they reveal something of the highest power the soul can find in itself once it has the certainty of being connected with the world of the spirit. Ernst von Feuchtersleben's words may be taken as a motto for everything connected with spiritual science: 'The human soul knows full well that in the final instance true happiness can only be gained by adding to its inner qualities and possessions.'

Adding to our inmost nature, gaining certainty and assurance in it – this is what the science of the spirit wants to offer to those who are engaged in the quest of our age.

LECTURE TWO

The Soul in the Light of Spiritual Science

Vienna, 8 April 1914

IT HAS BEEN FAR FROM EASY TO DISCUSS the basic principles of a science of the spirit such as the one we are representing – as has been done in the lecture given two days ago – but it would be fair to say that because of current habits of thinking and forming ideas, it is something of a risk to present the fruits of research which will be the subject of today's lecture. Because of those habits, some of the things I said two days ago must have seemed very strange, and understandably it may not be easy for you to accept that what I am going to say today represents serious scientific research. It is more than likely that many people will take this to be the ravings of an over-active mind. Anyone wishing to speak about these things must be fully aware of this situation and know that things which in a later age will be generally known – and indeed taken as a matter of course – will be considered highly peculiar and sheer fantasy when they are first presented.

This is said in advance, to show that the spiritual investigator is quite aware of the perfectly understandable reaction people may have to his findings.

Before I come to the actual findings, let me give you a brief outline of the basic inner attitude with which spiritual science is approached. It is utterly different from that used in other scientific disciplines. When it comes to understanding ordinary life and ordinary science today, we feel, with some justification, that we merely need to make our existing powers of understanding operative, as it were, to form an opinion on everything the physical world and natural science have to offer. In natural science all effort is directed into research, careful observation, and use of the intellect to discover the laws of nature. The mood in which a spiritual investigator sets out to gain insight and discover the truth is completely different. When you enter this field of research, you come to feel more and more that all inner work and research effort must first of all be devoted to preparation, and that you want to wait and to prepare yourself even better before you approach a particular truth in a particular area. You come to realize that the more work and effort you put into the path which has to be taken in the inner life before you do any actual research, the more will you be ready to receive the truth. For genuine spiritual research is a matter of receiving truths. This inner feeling or mood grows so strong that you feel overawed and reluctant to let these things come to you. Again and again you prefer to wait when it comes to gaining essential insights in spiritual research and not let them come to conscious awareness too early. As a result the spiritual investigator develops a very special mood which gradually spreads to all the inner work, such as the exercises of which I spoke two days ago, and brings an attitude of awe and almost dread with regard to the truth.

After these preliminary remarks I want to speak quite freely and openly on tonight's subject, which is of tremendous importance to every human soul. We cannot really blame the people who continue to insist that the truths of religious faith are distinct from those of scientific knowledge and that any ideas people may have regarding life beyond birth and beyond death can only be a matter of faith and cannot be proved by applying stringent scientific criteria. This division between faith and knowledge does not exist in the science of the spirit, and when we seek to evolve the truths that lie beyond death – which is what I intend to do today – we feel ourselves to be in harmony with things that have long been wanting to come into the modern life of the mind and intellect. You feel in harmony with this if you consider over and over again that the great Lessing[1] discussed one of the greatest truths spiritual science has to offer in the work he wrote shortly before his death, a work which represents the mature fruits of a thinking heart and mind. Lessing did not hesitate to say that the idea of repeated earth lives need not be wrong just because it was more or less one of the earliest ideas to arise in human minds, before the prejudices of scholasticism and of philosophers spread a veil which clouded the knowledge of the world beyond death, knowledge which people still had in the early days of civilization. When you base yourself on the science of the spirit you therefore feel in harmony – and it would be possible to quote many other great minds as well – with people who count among the best and whose efforts have contributed so much to human civilization.

Two days ago I said that to investigate the things and events connected with the life in the spirit, human beings must strengthen and enhance the powers which lie dormant in them, using the methods I described. Using the analogy of a chemist extracting hydrogen from water I said this enables the soul of the spiritual investigator to separate from the living physical body and know itself outside the body. The soul is then able to know the meaning of the words: 'I experience myself as a non-physical entity of soul and spirit outside the physical body; my body and everything belonging to it in the physical world is then like one of the objects in the world outside, that we can see with our eyes and touch with our hands.' On the last occasion when I was able to give public lectures here in Vienna, I spoke of the significant moment in the life of the spiritual investigator when he is truly ready, having done the exercises of which I have spoken – further information about these exercises may be found in my book *Knowledge of the Higher Worlds: How is it Achieved?* and in my *Occult Science: An Outline*. For the moment let me say what the spiritual investigator experiences in principle. When the point has been reached where the soul is able to go out of the body, the experience will come one day, or indeed one night, for either is possible, and if there has been the right kind of preparation the experience will cause no disruption in either of them. It may come in a hundred different ways and I will merely give you the essential character of it. It is as if you are waking from a sleep and know something is happening which is not a dream. It is removed from anything we perceive with the senses, all worries, passions and whatever the concerns of the day may be. Or it happens that in the midst of daily life you have to stop creating ideas in your mind and something entirely different comes into your conscious life of ideas. The nature of it will be something like this – I want to give you as concrete a picture as possible of this soul-stirring event experienced by the spiritual investigator. The nature of the feeling is as if you are a house that has been struck by lightning. Everything around you falls apart, like a house that has been struck by lightning. The lightning goes right through you. It feels as if the elements are taking away everything material connected with you and as if you are taken out of yourself, maintaining your self now as a spiritual entity. It is the deepest, most soul-stirring experience you can imagine. From this moment, or a similar one, you know what it means to find yourself in your soul out of the body. Throughout the ages spiritual investigators have used a term for this which seems very apt indeed to anyone who has had the experience. (Spiritual science has always existed, its form differing according to the particular civilization. Today's spiritual science differs from those of earlier times; it takes account of the advances made in modern natural science. What it is able to achieve, however, could also be achieved by the means available in other civilizations). The term used by spiritual investigators of many different ages for the experience I have just described is that you have arrived at the gate of death. And the experience which we would imagine to come with death does indeed come to us. It does not happen directly, as a reality, for the spiritual investigators return to their bodies and everything is as it was before – they once again perceive the world around them. But everything spiritual investigators experience is an image of what actually happens when human beings go through the gate of death; physical life comes to an end, and life after death begins.

To understand how spiritual investigators arrive at the things of which we are speaking, we have to realize that careful preparation of the inner life takes them to a point where they are able to perceive in a totally different way than we perceive with the ordinary senses. They are truly able to look into the spheres of existence of which we are going to speak.

The first thing to happen when one has gone through the kind of moment which takes one to the gate of death, may be defined by saying: You get to the other side of human memory. The power of memory may be said to be the very beginning of a spiritual element in us. This is also accepted by people involved in philosophical studies who know nothing about spiritual science. Bergson, the French philosopher who has done such brilliant work,[2] considers memory to be something purely of the spirit which has nothing to do with biological or physiological functions. Once the prejudices of modern science – which have got themselves so firmly attached to almost everybody at present – are a thing of the past, people will realize that the store of memories in the inner life marks the first stage of transition from things that are bound to the senses and the brain, to something that is pure inner life and spirit. When we push our ideas back down into memory, as it were, we do not preserve them by means of physical functions, but purely in the soul. I can only hint at this now, for it would take much time, and additional lectures, to present the scientific reasons for this. In everyday life, we perceive memory images which arise from the store of memories we hold. Because of the way they present themselves, there is nothing to induce us to treat them as illusions or hallucinations. The soul of the spiritual investigator perceives events and facts which are spiritual by nature. These do not come from the store of memories but from worlds of the spirit. One then finds it is possible to have experiences which lie behind the 'store of memories', as we call it. What the spiritual investigator sees is more or less as follows: Your soul has now been drawn out of your body and this means that you can now really look at the store of memories you have gained from the physical world, for it has become an object outside you. Yet this store of memories is like a veil which covers something which always lives in the soul, though it is unconscious. Human beings spread their memories out in the soul, and this subconscious element in soul and spirit is covered up. When spiritual investigators rise into the inner spiritual life, they do, of course, have their memories – which are attached to their inner spiritual life like the tail of a comet – but they are able to look through their memories and see something which we might call powers of a higher kind than the powers which preserve our memories. If the term were not so unpopular – and it is difficult to find suitable expressions for these things, which have no connection with the physical world – we might say: You rise from memory to super-memory. You gradually come to what we called 'forming imaginative ideas'. With memory, we always feel that when memory images come up and present themselves to the mind we are actually quite passive. But when you go deeper down and go behind your memory, you know you have to take an active part in producing the Imagination that seeks to come up as the content of a super-memory.

Having gone through the right kind of preparation, you also know that the super-memory has always been there and has merely been covered up by your memory. Perceiving its true nature you also know that the element which pushes its way down into the depths lying below the store of memories is itself actively working on our physical organism. You also make another discovery, one that is extremely important for the relationship of spiritual science to natural science. Natural scientists are saying today: Everything human beings feel, think and will is bound to the functions of the nervous system. This is correct. But natural science does not have the means to discover how the inner life is bound to the nervous system or, for example, how our thinking is tied to the brain. For this, we have to go to the much deeper foundations of the inner life. Spiritual science shows that in terms of our ordinary ideas of everyday life, and also in scientific work, it is quite correct to say that all the thoughts we produce and, for example, also our inner responses, are bound to the brain. The question is, how are they bound to the brain?

The deeper part of the soul, of which we know nothing in our ordinary consciousness and which is only discovered with the aid of spiritual science, initially works on, let us say, a particular part of the brain, sending its active forces into senses and brain. It is the work done by the inner life lying beyond conscious awareness which makes the nervous system into a mirror which reflects the events of everyday life. Mirror images of the inner life of soul and spirit present themselves in everyday life. It is just as if you were walking up to a mirror hanging on the wall; you would not be seeing yourself but a mirror image of yourself. This is exactly what you do when you think, form mental images, feel, and use your will in everyday life. The deeper part of the soul works specifically on the nervous system and the brain, and it is due to this work that we are able to have sensory perceptions. Work done on the eye, for example, makes the eye function in a particular way, reflecting colour into the inner life of soul and spirit.

Spiritual science will help people to realize that it is we ourselves who live in the mental images we form, and, with the aid of our deeper nature, prepare the body so that it becomes an apparatus reflecting our inner experiences. This is how it is in the ordinary life which is lived in space in the outside world.

Something else has to happen the moment our mental images become memory images. We have to pay attention; otherwise those images flit past like dreams. Anything to be preserved as a memory needs a longer period of concentration than, say, a mere mental image. A colour we have perceived would not stay in our memory if we looked at it only for as long as is needed to create the colour sensation. If we look at it for a longer time, we appeal to the power which keeps all such things in our souls as memories. We push our inner activity back, as it were, into a deeper part of our being, and this turns out to be not the physical body but something more subtle and ethereal than the physical body. 'Ether' is another term which is far from popular today, but the meaning it has in spiritual research is not the one it is usually given. The element, which is more subtle and ethereal than the physical body, is an etheric body which is spiritual by nature.

The soul not only creates memory images. Through its dealings with the outside world during the life between birth and death it also takes considerable activity into itself. But the strange thing we discover through spiritual science is that our memories remain mere images because they are held back by the ether body and not allowed to enter into the physical body. If they did enter into it and become active in it, they would seep into the powers which generate the physical body and give it life, and would completely organize the physical body. We let our mental images stay mental images and do not need to let them become organic functions. Thus their character as memories remains unchanged and we preserve their power as images.

The soul also develops powers in life which are much more powerful than those which create memories. Initially these powers are also kept in the soul, but they are kept behind the ordinary store of memories, so that they are like a super-memory in us. Spiritual investigators who are able to perceive the store of super-memories behind the ordinary memory then know the following: Something lives in your soul which cannot influence your physical body; it lies below the surface of your memory but does not take effect in the physical body as it is today, between birth and death. It does not stay a mental image, nor does it become a power acting on the organism. This is the experience spiritual investigators have when they are out of the body. They also experience the following, and once they are clear in their minds about this they are able to say: I experience something in my soul which is there but is not put to any use, as it were, for it cannot enter into the body which has developed from birth – or, let us say, conception – for there is no room for it. Entering wholly into this element, spiritual investigators gain living experience of it and come to know it just as we come to know the seed that forms in a plant. A plant develops all the way from root to fruit, and the fruit contains the seed, which therefore has been part of it from the beginning. The seed has no role to play in the plant, it cannot send its powers into the plant; instead, it is the germ of a plant that will follow, say, the year after. Spiritual investigation takes us into something which is a kernel, a seed in the soul, and we realize that this is produced in the present life between birth and death but does not unfold its powers in this life. It goes down into the deeper regions of the soul and lies there ready for a future life, just as the seed in a plant is there for a future plant that would not develop if it were not for the plant which precedes it.

When we know how to enter deeply into the realm of the soul, we reach understanding of the harmony that exists between successive lives on earth and the whole of the physical world outside us. It is important, however, that spiritual investigators never lose sight of the fact that the experiences they have to go through can only be such that they must over and over again be conscious of their own active involvement. If they are not, and if they fail to realize how these things have arisen, these experiences become illusory, hallucinatory, or mere figments of the imagination. It is quite wrong to say: Yes, but how can spiritual investigators know that the things they discover are not hallucinations, illusions and figments of the imagination? Surely they may well be hallucinations based on auto-suggestion? This objection would be perfectly justified if spiritual investigators were to take the attitude to these things that a diseased mind takes to hallucinations. For they come to us just like external objects perceived with the senses, and we cannot see through them. However, spiritual investigators have gone through the right preparation – you can read about it in my book *Knowledge of the Higher Worlds* – and are therefore able to differentiate between mere reminiscences of the outside world, and also figments of the imagination and hallucinations, to which we relate passively, and the things that present themselves in such a way that we realize, just as we do when we see letters or a word written on paper, that they are not what they look like, but something else. Spiritual investigators do not use the things they perceive in the same way as people use hallucinations, but in a way that may be compared with the mind reading something written in the Imaginations which present themselves. We have to learn to use the things we put before the mind through our own activities from choice and in such a way that we live in them, just as we live in something written, seeing through it and perceiving what it means. We have to gain this kind of inner strength through development and thus attain to inner vision; only then will we truly perceive events and entities which belong to the world of the spirit. We then gradually come to be at home in the element of our inner life which is not identical with the body, and find the part of ourselves of which we may say that it has the quality of immortality.

Spiritual science is not a speculative form of philosophy where you consider the possible reasons for immortality of soul. Spiritual science shows you how to reach the soul itself and then reveals the real nature of this true soul. It lays the soul bare, as it were, and you then find that the soul is not a product of the physical body, but rather that the body is the product of the soul principle you discover. On the one hand we discover the kernel of the soul and are able to feel and experience this as the seed for a future life on earth. On the other hand, in becoming conscious of contents that lie above the store of memory, we also experience the essence of the physical body which enters into human beings before they enter into physical existence at birth, or, let us say, conception.

When we perceive with the senses,[3] the soul itself prepares the brain, in terms of space, so that the brain reflects its contents. We also discover that the element of soul and spirit to which we have penetrated existed in a world of the spirit before our birth and conception. There it gained the powers it needed to unite with the physical substance provided by the father and the mother, to take this substance into itself and organize it so that it would suit its needs. We find that when human beings come into the world, they are not merely the offspring of a father and a mother, but that the spiritual principle unites with the physical material provided by the parents, having itself come from worlds of the spirit where it lived between the last death and the present conception.

Discovering the part of the soul which lies beyond our memory we also come to realize what the soul is like when the physical body no longer inhibits the activities of soul and spirit, which is when death has come for the human being. When this has happened, the reality shown through spiritual science is that the soul first of all lives in the part which has not become physical during life on earth – in the store of memories. During the first stages after death, a wide panorama of memories relating to everything experienced between birth and death opens out before the human being. This takes just a few days. Spiritual investigators are able to understand this first after-death experience because they know the true nature of the memory. When the soul is out of the body, spiritual investigators can enter into conscious experience of something which we experience when we have gone through the gate of death. When they are out of the body, their whole thought-content presents itself, but now as a whole world. Normally we have mountains, clouds, stars, sun, moon, rivers and cities around us; when we are out of the body, we first of all gain a panoramic view of everything we have experienced. But we are able to see through it and perceive its power to act. Once you have got accustomed to seeing through these things when out of the body, you gradually also gain the ability to direct your attention deliberately to what the soul lives through after death, what it has lived through after your last death and what will come after the death which lies ahead. First of all the panorama of memories spreads out before you. Yet behind this appears another power of the soul. When death lies behind you, this power is no longer inhibited by the body; it takes effect, causing the memory images to disappear after a few days.

As I said at the beginning, speaking about the subject of today's lecture is a venture involving some risk, but we have to touch on these things if we are talk of more than just generalities. I have tried to show what has been discovered through spiritual research concerning this first after-death experience. It has been found that this review of memory images relating to experiences from the last life takes a different length of time with different people; it takes longer for some, and less time for others. Generally speaking, it takes about as long as the time for which the individual would have been able to stay awake if prevented from going to sleep in the life which now lies behind. Some people can hardly keep awake for a single night, others for many nights. The inner power to overcome sleep is the measure for the number of days for which the review will continue before something else takes its place.

The new element is something we can only really enter into if we know it already from out-of-body experience. It is extremely difficult to find words for this, for these experiences are utterly different from those we have in everyday life. Our language has been created for the physical world; anything outside this world is experienced in a totally different way. Forgive me, therefore, if some of the words and phrases I use seem awkward or even paradoxical. I can assure you that when one tries to use ordinary words to describe something which is difficult to put in words, it is impossible to describe how experiences which follow the memory review present themselves to the soul. The things the soul of the spiritual investigator now experiences when out of the body are something I want to call 'feeling combined with will', or 'will combined with feeling', for it is somewhere between the two. It is a power we develop; we do not have it in everyday life. Spiritual investigators know it. It is as if the will moves along with us in the world; and as if this will, as it moves, bears on its wings, or waves, a feeling element that comes as if from outside, coming towards us on the waves of the will. We normally experience our feelings as something with which we have inwardly grown together, but now it becomes something which surges and actively moves on the waves of the will. At the same time we know that because we spread out into the world as we experience this, so that the will combined with feeling, or feeling combined with will, is out there in the same way as colours and sounds are perceived outside us in the physical world, our own true nature has entered into it. There is a feeling out there that we perceive in the way we perceive light; but at the same time we also feel connected with it.

Initially after the memory review, the experience is that the only world which can be perceived is the world we left behind at death. When the panorama has faded, this feeling combined with will, or will combined with feeling, unfolds and increases in power in the soul. However, it will only bring things to expression which are connected with our last life on earth. The things we experience may therefore be characterized more or less as follows: Life on earth never allows human beings to experience everything it really has to offer. Many things remain such that we may say: We have not taken in everything we might have taken in and which could have made an impression on us between birth and death. Something by way of desires, wishes, love for others, and so on, had to remain between the lines of life. The spirit now looks back with desire to things left undone, and it does so for years. These are the years when our world consists mainly of what we have been. We look into our last existence on earth and see what has been left undone. We have to live for years in a sphere where none of this can be brought to a satisfactory conclusion in the way it can be brought to a conclusion on earth, because we have laid aside the physical organs which would enable us to do so. Thus we gradually work our way through the things that tie us to our last life on earth.

Again, spiritual science must consider the time taken up by these experiences, and we are able to say the following: The period of early childhood, up to the time to which our memory is able to go back, does not affect the time taken by the experience I have described. Nor does the time we live through after our twenty-fifth, twenty-sixth or twenty-seventh year. The years from about the fourth year of life until we are in our twenties indicate the length of time during which we are still connected with the last life on earth and have to gather experiences from that life and withdraw from it. Spiritual investigation shows that the time taken to find our way out of the last life on earth is about as long as the time we took after our previous life in the spirit to build up our bodies, as it were, with the powers which follow an upward trend until we reach the mid-twenties. It is as long as the time it took us to fill life with physical powers, powers that are fruitful at the organic level and powers that bring desire and the seeking of rewards. Anyone who lived to the age of twelve, say, would only need between five and seven years to leave the last life on earth behind. Yet if someone has lived to the age of fifty, the years beyond the mid-twenties will not be added on to this particular period.

To some extent human beings will begin to perceive spiritual events and entities around them when they have gone through this for some time. As I have mentioned before, spiritual investigators are in a real world of the spirit when they experience themselves in soul and spirit. The dead enter into that world, but initially they are so much occupied with the previous world, in the way we have discussed, that they can only relate to their new surroundings by a roundabout route which goes through the previous world they knew. Let me give you an example. Someone has gone through the gate of death and completed the review. He is now living in the period where he tears himself free from anything relating to his life on earth. Someone whom he loved is still in the physical body. The human being who is still at the stage of which we have been speaking cannot make a direct connection with the person who is still on earth. But a kind of relay system develops: in the last life on earth we loved the person who has been left behind; and when we are at the stage under discussion we turn to the love we have felt. Our feelings are our environment at that time. Looking at them we find the way to the person who is still on earth.

We also have to go via our feelings when we want to find the way to a soul that has gone through the gate of death. Thus we can say: After death the human being lives with human souls, but initially by a roundabout route taken through one's own life.

Gradually a power develops in the soul which spiritual investigators also know when they experience themselves in soul and spirit outside the body. There is now no way of expressing this. We were at least able to call the last power discussed 'will combined with feeling', or 'feeling combined with will', because it has some similarity with the will and with feeling. The will impulses and feelings have become external objects, but the things which surge out there as elements of will and feeling still have some similarity with the impulses of will combined with feeling that we have in ordinary life.

Now, however, the soul is getting further and further away from the last life on earth, and experiences a power coming to life in it which I can only describe in terms that may sound clumsy, but are nevertheless to the point: creative power of the soul. This now comes to direct experience. The soul very much finds itself entering into an activity and at the same time finds that this creative power truly develops, radiating from the soul into the environment and – again a clumsy way of putting it, but I will have to use the term in order to make myself understood – this power shines out into the environment like a light of the spirit; it illuminates the events and entities around us, so that we are able to see them.

When the sun rises we see the objects around us; in the same way our own inner power of light pours out and we see the events and entities in the world of the spirit. The term used in religious life to describe life after death is not inappropriate. This state where we feel ourselves to have creative power, getting to be at home in a spiritual environment that becomes visible as we send our own creative powers into it, this experience of the outpouring of light is a feeling of bliss. Even pain is experienced as bliss in this world, where the soul now goes through further experiences.

It has to be realized that the soul can only go through this experience in alternating states. (This takes us into realms which are utterly fantastic in terms of ordinary life. But having said what I did say in preparation, I can now also come to these things. It has to be clearly understood that spiritual investigators will never say anything other than that such things can only come to them when they live out of the body.) The soul, then, is not always in the state where the power of spiritual light shines out from it, where human souls and spiritual entities are around it, and it experiences spiritual events. This state must alternate with one where the soul feels that the radiance of the spirit coming from it dies down. The soul grows dull inside and can no longer illuminate its surroundings; it has to take all that it is back into itself. Now comes the moment when the soul lives a completely solitary life in the time between death and rebirth, and this takes a long time. If we wanted to compare it with ordinary life, we may say that in ordinary life human beings alternate between sleeping and waking, and after death they must alternate between a life that pours out into the outside world and a life of inner solitude. Then everything previously experienced as being spread out is gathered in, and the soul knows: You are now entirely by yourself. In sleep, we become unconscious; here, we withdraw into ourselves but do not lose consciousness. The soul's conscious awareness is in fact heightened during the periods of solitude and the experience is such that the soul knows: Outside is the world of the spirit, but you are by yourself; everything you experience now you experience inside yourself. Those experiences are the echoes of what the soul experienced when it was outside. It needs this so that the power of light may grow strong and shine out once more. You then wake up again, as it were, in the spirit and experience the other state.

It is a very strange experience when you actually have to learn to connect a meaning with the words that between death and rebirth the soul lives a sociable life with other spirits and then lives in solitude, and that this alternation between sociability and solitude, which however, takes much longer than day and night, is something similar in life after death as sleeping and waking are in physical life. I made some mention of this in my penultimate book.[4] But as it lives on between death and rebirth the soul finds that the power of its light is gradually fading. We might say that the experiences of inner solitude grow stronger and stronger, gradually reaching the point where the human being experiences a whole inner world, an inner cosmos. It really is the case that the human being is overcome with something like fear of himself when he discovers all the things that are now, about halfway between death and rebirth, emerging from the depths of the soul.

Then comes a time which I have tried to present in my fourth Mystery Play, *The Soul's Awakening*.[5] It is a time when human beings can only have inner experiences, with the nights of solitude growing longer and longer; they are no longer able to wake in the spirit to an awareness where the power of light radiates out from them. I have tried to express this experience by using the symbolic term: the midnight hour of existence in the spirit between death and rebirth. Then human beings have their world in everything which lies in the depths of their souls and only know: Beyond the shores of your soul are the worlds of the spirit; there all the spiritual entities are to be found, and all human souls, both in and out of the body, and all other entities. They only know of this because they have its echoes in them.

Then something arises in the soul which again cannot be fully described by an ordinary word. In ordinary language, 'longing' is the most passive element in the soul. We are more passive when we have longings in physical life than we are in anything else. We long for something, desire something we do not have – and our longing certainly will not produce the object for which we long. We can only be entirely passive. However, powers of soul take on a completely different character when the soul is out of the body. Out of the depths of solitude, out of the soul's experience at the cosmic midnight hour of the spirit, arises the longing to live in the world again from which our solitude has taken us. This longing grows active and turns into a spiritual reality, an organizing power. It truly becomes a new power of perception. Longing in the spirit gives birth to a new inner power, one that is able to perceive an outside world, though this is both an outside and an inside world. It is an outside world because it truly exists outside our own self, and an inside world because we see it as the world of everything we lived through when we were last incarnated on earth. Because of our longing, this then becomes our outside world. We look at all the things which were left undone in that previous life, and our longing fashions powers in us to balance out the bad, stupid and ugly things we did, when we are in a new life.

This is the time when every human being is able to look back over previous earth lives, seeing, with eyes of the spirit, everything that was done in those lives, and the inclination arises to balance these things out in a new life on earth, completing and making good the experiences gone through in earlier lives.

I have known people who said that one life was enough for them, and I even knew a man who came close to thinking repeated earth lives a sensible idea – only he then sent a postcard from the nearest railway station to say that he did not want to know about another life on earth after all. However, it does not matter whether we can have an idea of repeated earth lives or not; what matters is that at the point of which I am speaking every soul looks back on earlier earth lives and at the same time receives the inclination to live a new life on earth that will balance out earlier lives. You also find there are people to whom you owe something or who owe something to you, and the inclination develops to share life again with the people to whom you owe something, so that the debt may be paid. Other people develop the same inclination. This awakens inner powers in a number of people who previously lived at the same time and these powers incline them towards the earth. The result is that people who were together before, come together again on earth. The things they owe each other need to be balanced out. These inclinations gain in power and come increasingly more alive as life between death and rebirth continues, and human beings create the spiritual idea, the archetype, of their new life on earth out of what they have learned about their earlier lives.

Human beings themselves create the new life that will unite with the physical substance given by the father and the mother. Depending on the nature of that physical substance and its affinity to the spiritual idea, this spiritual idea is drawn towards the physical substance before conception occurs, and we may say that the elective affinity between inherited qualities and the archetype decides who the parents will be to whom the soul feels drawn as if by a magnet, and also decides the kind of life one finds for oneself. This is how the human being returns to earth and unites again with a physical body. Spiritual science shows the mystery of childhood development – anyone who knows how to observe childhood life will find this to be true – when facial expression gradually emerges, dexterous movements develop from clumsy movements, and the powers that are so obviously at work inside shape and model the body. Spiritual investigators see how something which has gone through the experiences that come between death and rebirth, and of which I have spoken, unites more and more with the living body.

They are now able to see why initially there can be no memories of pre-birth experiences: The powers which have the capacity to become powers of memory are used to organize the living body. Children could indeed remember everything that has gone before, for they have the powers, but these powers are transformed. When I run my finger across the surface of this table, the powers of friction are transformed into heat. In the same way those powers of memory are transformed into organizing powers. Transformed powers which go back to the past inwardly organize the whole of the child's body and give shape and form to the brain, so that the child will later be able to think and to develop powers of memory in the physical body. The form in which these powers were able to develop the panoramic review disappears and they organize the whole of the body. The spiritual principle that organizes the body is a transformed soul principle which has flowed into the body. We understand the life in which we are now if we understand what happened outside this life and beyond death. The principle which is active in life on earth has gained its powers between death and rebirth. The powers which were then purely of the spirit are transformed powers of memory which flow into the body and organize the whole of it.

One day scientists will discover that the powers which are entirely dedicated to heredity also go through a process of being created in the human being at the time when the power of reproduction develops. Certain lower animals die as soon as they are mature enough to give birth to another animal. The powers human beings must develop in order to have physical offspring and pass things on to them through heredity, must be fully developed when sexual maturity is reached. I can only mention this briefly. Natural science and spiritual science together will be able to provide important insights in this field. Spiritual principles are, however, active in everything that is physical power in human beings. Powers of spirit are active in the physical body, penetrating every part of it. The physical body is like a reflection of the spiritual principle. Fundamentally speaking, the processes which allow the body to function as a mirror are destructive processes. When we see colours or hear sounds, this always involves destructive processes, and we also produce destructive processes inside us when we produce memory images. And people need to sleep, for otherwise only destructive processes would be active in them.

We live by letting powers we have acquired outside the body penetrate this body and give it powers. Life can only be understood if we consider the element of soul and spirit which is active in life.

Things are not as simple in spiritual science as they are in other fields of study, and we cannot speak of the death of plants and animals in the same way as we do of the death of human beings. Everything I have said today applies only to human beings, and we see that spiritual science extends our horizons beyond birth and death. Even details find an explanation. I can well imagine that the ladies and gentlemen in the audience who have some interest in the findings of spiritual research would like to hear some details. I can, however, only give a few of these details today.

The first example is one that, paradoxical as this may seem, will strike even spiritual investigators as a real mystery in life. It is the existence of criminal characters. The view held in spiritual science certainly is not that criminals deserve nothing but our compassion and should not be punished. It is not the business of spiritual investigators to meddle in the outer affairs of the world, but they do want to understand the things we find in human life, and they want to do so out of the depths of the world of the spirit. So we ask ourselves: What is the situation when a life turns out to be criminal? Well, it is easy to say this, but it is a struggle to find the answers to questions like these and essentially also a struggle to talk about them, for they seem very strange indeed in the light of present-day ideas.

If clairvoyant vision is directed towards the criminal element, we find that criminals are born prematurely, as it were, in a spiritual sense. Every soul has the 'normal' opportunity to come down from the worlds of the spirit and unite with physical substance. The inclinations which lead to this interact with other inclinations, however, so that most people – and especially criminals – come into life on earth earlier than they should. This is the strange discovery we make.

Something else happens as a result. It is only possible to enter fully into the living body and be a full human being on earth if you reincarnate at approximately the normal time. If there are reasons to come down to earth earlier, because of events in earlier lives, you bring something with you which lives in the subconscious and of which you are not consciously aware. In the depths of the soul lies something that is rather like not taking life seriously, because the individual has not come to earth at the time when it would have been possible to unite most fully with the physical body. The bond is therefore only a superficial one. People are not aware of this, however. It is then possible to have an abnormally developed instinct for self-preservation at the upper level of the conscious mind, so that the individual is hostile towards the social world, develops an extreme egotism and becomes a criminal. Yet inwardly — and this is not known — the criminal may have a tendency to be superficial and not take life seriously, putting no value on it. This is due to premature birth in the spirit. The individual concerned may then also fire the overdeveloped instinct of self-preservation with the unconscious tendency not to take life seriously, and you see this grow and flourish in criminal characters.

Once I realized this, something else became clear to me. A dictionary of thieves' cant has been published, and you really only understand this form of language, where life is not taken seriously and words are used that come from the subconscious level of the soul, when you know the things I have just mentioned. It must always be pointed out, however, that in the totality of earth lives, the crimes of one life are made up for, and it is exactly because they experience the consequences of their criminal activities that criminals progress to other earth lives where things are balanced out.[6]

Other things also become clearer when we consider the mysteries of life in the light of spiritual science. We see people die in an accident or disaster, for instance. Oddly enough we find that if people die from such causes at a time when they otherwise would not yet have left the earth, that is, when their physical powers still extend beyond the time of death, ...[7] When someone is run over by a steam locomotive at the age of thirty-four, for instance, someone who is not seeking to take his own life, his body still holds powers that could have become active. When the individual leaves the physical world, those powers do not vanish into nothingness; instead, the investigator sees that the element of soul and spirit, the powers of intelligence and the powers of thinking things out more accurately may actually be enhanced because of that very accident. The individual concerned may be reborn with greater powers of intelligence than someone who has died a natural death.

You have to accept the fact that spiritual science, which considers life within a wide horizon, has to present many things differently from the way in which they are presented in everyday life. Someone who dies relatively early, from a disease, say, and who has gone through a lot because of this disease, has prepared the soul in such a way that powers of will may be enhanced. Dying early from a disease enhances the powers of will.

Some of these things may seem quite unbelievable. Perhaps you will permit me to say, however, that I am conscious of my responsibility in speaking about them. I would not discuss them if I did not know the means by which they can be known with the same certainty in spiritual science as objects in the outside world can be known. I would consider it frivolous in the extreme to say such things, unless one has inner knowledge and says them in the kind of mood I have just indicated.

Understanding of human life is thus gained from things that are outside physical life. The life which evolves between birth and death is the outcome of the life which lies beyond birth and death. Some may feel that this lessens the value of life. Let me briefly repeat the following, so that none of you may feel like this. Someone may say: You tell us that we ourselves have prepared the events we experience during life on earth. This is true. But when we are in an accident we are in it because we have originally implanted the inclination in the soul to get involved in the accident. Alpine plants, which do not thrive in lowland plains, seek out high altitudes. In the same way the human soul seeks out a situation where it will be involved in an accident; it grows into what it then experiences as destiny. It is the natural destiny of those plants to grow in the Alps. It is natural for a human soul to plunge into misfortune, for the inclination to do so has come with the insight that overcoming such a misfortune will make the soul more perfect in a particular respect, whilst it would have to remain less perfect if it did not have that misfortune.

People may say: This means we forge our own misfortunes, and it is no consolation to be told not only that we should suffer and endure our misfortunes but that we have, in a sense, earned them in the world of the spirit. The answer must be, and I have shown this before, using an analogy: When a young man has lived a well-do-to life paid for out of his father's pocket until he was in his eighteenth year, has not learnt anything during those years and his father then goes bankrupt, this may appear to be a great misfortune, for life will be hard. Quite rightly, our young man would now find life a misery. Let us assume, however, that at the age of fifty he looks at life from a different point of view and says to himself: I would not be what I am today if I had not fallen into misfortune then. It has been a misfortune for my father, but for me it was the leaven that allowed life to develop.

We are not always in a position to see our misfortunes from the right point of view when we are caught up in them. Before we are born, our point of view is entirely different from what it is afterwards; it is that the experiences of a new life must balance out the things which happened before. We then prepare for ourselves the misfortune that we will be right to accept and suffer later on, and about which we are also right to complain, because at the time we see it only from the point of view of what happens in physical life on earth.

There are a few more things I should like to say about the time between death and rebirth. I have already mentioned the brief period of review which comes after death; it is only a matter of days. The period that follows takes longer; it is a matter of decades. Spiritual investigators use something like the following method to establish the length of this period. In order to develop the powers they need to gain insight into such things they must first of all ask themselves: When you are out of the body, which element in your soul presents itself to you as something which the soul can take with it through death? Strangely, the experience they get is that on this occasion something is taken out of the body, whilst normally everything is left behind. When spiritual investigators leave the body, they leave behind their passions, memories, and so on, but they take with them all efforts made to overcome difficulties. This is something we can only gain after reaching the twenties, let us say. People will not be pleased to hear this, for nowadays young people are considered capable of even the highest things before they have reached their twentieth year. Yet the truth is that when we really have experiences because of what we are, and in such a way that they become a store of wisdom, this happens because we have already gained other experience and look back on this when new experiences come. The inner experiences gained as we work our way up inwardly by our own effort lay the first foundations for the experiences the soul will have between death and rebirth. The soul must therefore live in constant effort, overcoming obstacles and transforming powers. As a rule it then remains in the world between death and rebirth for as long as anything still remains to be transformed.

From another aspect we may say the following: We grow into a particular time, taking in and learning things as members of a particular tribe or nation. When we went through death we used this to create life experiences. But the earth changes, and not only in its physical aspect. Perhaps members of the audience will be so kind and think themselves back into the time, say, when Christianity was founded, to consider what the area where Vienna is today may have looked like then. However, the signs of civilization on the face of the earth, which are the spiritual element in our environment from which we gain our store of memories, change within even shorter periods of time. Souls normally only return to earth for a new life when they are able to find a completely new spiritual environment. We find that souls are not reborn at random, but in a way which enables them to gain new experiences. This means they have to change everything they knew in the last life on earth; for instance the ability to express themselves in a particular language. They have to acquire new language skills. This is a time-scale which goes in hundreds of years. It normally takes something like 1000 or 1500 years. But, as I said, under certain circumstances people may be born prematurely in the spirit.

Time is getting short and I cannot go into more detail. Do let me say, however, that if any of you were inclined to go home feeling: All this is really quite unbelievable; surely he cannot claim to know these things! you should recall what I said at the beginning, which is that in the past, too, things which later on would be taken for granted, with everybody knowing about them, seemed strange indeed when they were first told. Anyone involved in the science of the spirit today has to accept that people will quite understandably consider things sheer fantasy which later will be accepted as surely as the ideas put forward by Copernicus have come to be accepted, even though in the beginning many people thought them to be sheer fantasy and even harmful. Let me mention once more the image that spiritual investigators and people who are able to understand the science of the spirit call to mind to make them conscious of the truth that will gradually win the day. This truth may have to squeeze through extremely narrow clefts, with powerful rock masses of prejudice pressing down on it, but it will win through. It helps to strengthen this awareness if we remember Giordano Bruno.[8] He shattered prejudices which were hundreds of years old, saying: People believed that when they looked up into the wide space yonder, the blue vault of heaven spread above them, sun and planets would have their orbits in it, with the blue vault of heaven being a wall, a blue wall. Giordano Bruno said: This wall merely appears to you because that is as far as your powers of perception will go. You have created your own limit, but it does not really exist. Infinities of space extend out there. And those infinities of space are filled with an infinity of worlds.

Today spiritual investigators have to remember that human

vision has expanded into the infinities of space, and that it was Giordano Bruno who first pointed out that the limits set by the vault of heaven were merely the limits of human powers of perception; they have to point out that the time-limits set for human experience are another such firmament. When we consider human life with our physical organs of perception and with the intellect, we see the limits marked by birth and death, just as people in the past saw the limit set by the blue vault of heaven, a limit which did not exist. The limit set for human experience between birth – or let us say conception – and death owes its existence to the limited human powers of perception. Beyond birth, or conception, and beyond death lies an infinity of time, with repeated human lives on earth and lives between death and rebirth embedded in it and extending both backwards and forwards. I cannot tell you everything about those repeated lives: how they once had a beginning, and that human beings were born out of the spirit and found their dwelling place here on earth – the earth itself evolved out of the world of the spirit at that time – and that a time will come when human beings will have gone through their repeated lives on earth, the earth itself will drop away and they will enter into a different form of life, one which will again be in the spirit. I can only mention this briefly; details can be found in my *Occult Science*.

The work done in the science of the spirit may be going against the mainstream of present-day thinking, but we are nevertheless able to say that leading thinkers of the past – I concluded the lecture I gave two days ago in the same way – did have an inkling of the ideas that are now coming to life again in the science of the spirit. They did not have this science in the form in which I have presented it to you, for it is a child of our time and will develop out of the education which people have today. But individuals who in the past knew themselves in their hearts to be united with the spirit of the cosmos, the spirit that is active and alive in all human beings, put thoughts into words that we, in the science of the spirit, can wholeheartedly agree with. The science of the spirit shows us how we can understand life between birth and death by perceiving the immortal element, which also lives in a world of the spirit, as it is active and alive in our physical bodies and in the whole of physical life. It shows us that we have life when in our bodies because of the life we have when out of the body. No one can therefore understand life between birth and death unless they also understand life outside this [physical] firmament.[9] Goethe, who clearly had an inkling of what our science of the spirit would reveal, put this in words which give a clear indication not only of his belief in immortality, but also of his awareness that insight gained into the present life, and experience of it, has true value only if we know that immortal life fills our life on earth with its fire, light and activity. Let us therefore sum up the knowledge gained through our science of the spirit, which is, that a true inner reality of mortal life is found through immortal life,[10] and our present inner response to this knowledge, in words that were once used by Goethe: 'To those who are not at all willing to consider the particular character of the present life in order to arrive at an idea of another life, I' – these are Goethe's words – 'would say, with Lorenzo de Medici, that all those who do not hope for another life are dead also with regard to this life.'[11]

LECTURE THREE

The Four Spheres of the Inner Life

Vienna, 9 April 1914

THE AIM OF THIS COURSE OF LECTURES WILL BE to describe the inner life in relation to the life between death and a new birth, in order to show the close relationship between these two realms of existence. This should enable us to develop guiding principles that will help us to find our bearings in many difficult situations. By gaining a real understanding of the inner life we can achieve the stability this life needs. It will be necessary for you to work steadily through the first lectures, which are intended to provide a foundation. They will take us into domains of esoteric science which may seem far removed from the kind of knowledge that our hearts and minds may tell us we would like to have immediately. However, once we have achieved the aim of these lectures, you will realize that the only safe and sure way of getting there was to work our way through the seemingly remote esoteric knowledge which will now be presented to you.

If you take an abstract view of the inner life you will find that it has three distinct aspects – thinking, feeling and our will impulses. However, a fourth element has to be added, which consists of our inner reactions to sensory experiences. You see, we do not merely let colours and sounds, the experience of different temperatures and so on, dart past the conscious mind, but we lay hold of them and take note of them. We are able to remember them and keep them in mind, and are thus able to know that a rose is red not only when we see it. We can carry the red colour of the rose around with us and store it and other colours in our memories. This serves to show that our inner reactions, the things we note and through which we relate to the outside world, are also part of the inner life. Anything we note in the outside world is part of our inner life because we make it so.

Through the world of thought we acquire knowledge of our immediate surroundings and, in science, of objects which are more remote. We use thought to make the outside world part of our inner world in a much wider sense than through sensory perception. We do not merely take note of things but think about them, and we are aware that this uncovers some of the secrets of the things we perceive.

Emotions and feelings are another part of our inner life. Our feelings are the part of our inner life through which we are in touch with the outside world in a way that is in accord with the dignity of man. The fact that we are able to feel things and take pleasure in our surroundings is the real basis of our being truly human, and to some extent this also makes up the joys and pain of life. All this takes place in the rise and fall of our feelings. Feelings arise in us which heighten the quality of life, so that we are happy and content and gain strength. Other feelings bring pain and suffering; they come to us through life's events, through destiny and also from our inner life. When we speak of 'feelings' or 'emotions' we refer to a realm which does indeed hold all the happiness and pain of human life.

The fourth element, the will, is something which makes us of value to the world. It makes us part of the world, so that we do not merely live in our own perceptions and feelings but are able to leave our mark on the world. All the will impulses of which human beings are capable represent our true value to the world when they progress from will intent to action. In the realm of the will, therefore, the human being is part of the world, and it is our inner life which streams into the world and becomes part of it.

It is immaterial at this point if the egotistical, antisocial urges and passions of a criminal mind enter into the will and from there into the world and cause destruction, or the high-minded pure ideals which idealists gain from being in touch with a higher world order and which enter into their actions, or perhaps even only their words, so that they may fire the minds of others or perhaps have an effect by revealing the dignity of man. In either case, anything to do with the will gives human beings their value.

All the richness for which our inner life holds the potential can therefore be brought to expression in these four spheres: sensory perception, thinking, feeling and will impulses.

If we now take a deeper look at these four spheres of inner human nature, a significant difference can be seen between the first two and the last two of these. This is something of which we are not much aware in ordinary life; at best we can become aware of it by considering it in the following way.

When we talk about taking note of things and reflect on this, we may get the feeling that here we are in direct connection with the outside world. We make this world part of our inner life when we work on our inner reactions to it. We also feel that our reactions must be such as to give us true pictures of the outside world. If there is any abnormality in sensory perception, in our reactions and in the senses themselves, it is evident that this impoverishes the inner life, for we then receive less from the outer world.

If we now move on from sensory perception to thinking, we may be aware that it is not enough for our thinking to delve around in itself and focus on itself only. When all is said and done, our thoughts only have value for us if they bring something objective, something from outside ourselves to our awareness and if they can throw a light on it. It would give us no satisfaction to think about things unless this taught us something about the outside world.

When we think about our emotions and feelings, we find that the life of feeling is much more closely connected with our own inner being than are thinking and sensory perception. We gain the idea that we must go through further development – to begin with entirely on the physical plane – before we will be able to sense and get the right feeling for some of the more subtle aspects of the outside world. If we have an idea and take note of this, we say that if the thought is true it must also ring true to all other human beings; we need only find the right words and it should be possible to convince others of its truth. When we are faced with a natural phenomenon or a work of art and develop feelings about it, we know that, fundamentally speaking, our human nature, such as it is, will not help us to fathom completely what we have in front of us. It is quite possible to be completely untouched by a piece of music or a painting, simply because we have not educated our feelings to the point where we can perceive its subtleties. If we pursue this further we find that the life of feeling is deeply inward and we cannot easily express what we feel in thoughts which can be shared with others. In the life of feelings we are always on our own, though we also know it to be a source of a particular inner richness and real inner development exactly because it is highly subjective and cannot enter directly into outside objects, at least not the way it is.

The same must be said with regard to the will. Just think how different we are from each other when it comes to the will impulses that may arise and to what we are capable of doing in the world thanks to our will. Human actions come in such rich variety exactly because one of us intends to do one thing and another one something different.

Think of the joy we feel when we have found someone who inwardly, purely subjectively, has come to the same point of view in the realm of feeling as we ourselves, someone whose feelings allow him to make some of the more subtle aspects of the outside world his own in such a way that his understanding of it is quite independent of us and yet also connected with us. The quality of life is enhanced by such companionship. The life of feeling is an inward one, yet it is possible for two people to harmonize in their feelings.

There cannot be two will impulses directed to one and the same objective, that is, two people who want to do the same thing at the same time. Two wills cannot unite in a single objective. Only one of us can grasp the handle that will turn the machine, and if someone gives us a hand, the part we do out of our own will is only half of the whole job that has to be done; we do our half and the other person is doing the other half. Two will impulses cannot unite in one objective. We can be part of a common world through the will, but this happens in such a way that each of us is a single individual because of the will. We see therefore that the will constitutes the whole individual value of a person and from this point of view it is the most inward part of us.

Perception and thought are therefore more on the outside of our inner life, whilst feeling and will are the most deeply inward and indeed our essential inner nature.

Another difference emerges when we consider these four spheres of the inner life in a perfectly ordinary and non-esoteric way.

As we perceive the world around us we are bound to say to ourselves: Perception does bring the world to us, but always only from a single point of view. The part of the world we are thus able to make part of our inner life is extremely limited, and it is always dependent on place and time. It has to be said that sensory perception provides only the smallest part of all we divine the world to be. With regard to our thoughts we have the feeling that no matter what efforts we make there are always further steps to be taken; our thinking can always lead us on and on. In short, we realize that the world is there outside, and with perception and thinking we can only make a tiny portion of it our own.

It is different with feeling, for here we say to ourselves: What infinite possibilities of feeling, of joy and sorrow, are there within me! What could I not bring forth from the depths of my soul! And if I did so, my feelings about the world would be much finer and of a higher order. With regard to perception and thought we feel we can only gain access to a very small part of the rich abundance the world has to offer. With regard to feeling, we have to realize that there are infinite depths, and if we were to be able to draw on these our feelings would be ever richer and richer. We can only draw on a minute part and transform this into actual feeling. This also applies to the will, and to a far higher degree. Let me mention just one thing. Think of how much we are aware that in our achievements we fall far short of our true potential.

We realize, therefore, that perception and thinking bring only part of the outside world into our inner life, and that our feeling and will impulses are only part of what lies deep down in the soul. The four spheres of the inner life thus fall into two categories — perception and thinking on the one hand, feeling and will on the other.

Quite a different light is thrown on these four spheres when we try to bring esoteric insight to bear on the insights we have gained.

We know that at night, when we are asleep, the connection between the ego and the astral body on the one hand and the physical and ether bodies on the other hand is different from the connection which exists when we are awake. In the daytime, physical body, ether body, astral body and ego may be said to be coupled together in the normal way. During sleep, the connection is loosened, with the astral body and the ego outside the sphere of the senses and of thinking — in other words, the whole sphere of the instruments of consciousness. To begin with, therefore, the darkness of night spreads over normal consciousness, and unconsciousness takes its place. If individuals strengthen their inner faculties by esoteric exercises so that the entity of soul and spirit which is unconscious and outside the body during the night gains the faculty of spiritual perception and cognition, and if they genuinely experience this entity of soul and spirit as their human nature, a new, spiritual environment opens up to them, just as we have a physical environment around us when we are using our senses and the brain as our instrument of thinking.

The world of the spirit we are then able to observe is by no means the same on every occasion. People can take on the role of spiritual investigator at different times and in different ways. The investigators' purposes or intentions, what they desire to know, will always be a factor in what they perceive in the spirit. I do not mean the conscious purpose but the more unconscious and instinctive purpose. If we leave the body, for instance, to make contact with someone who has died, this purpose will affect the whole field of our spiritual consciousness. We shall be blind to anything that has no connection with this purpose. If the investigator succeeds at all, he will steer straight for the dead person and his destiny so that he may behold exactly what he desires to behold in connection with the dead person. The rest of the spiritual world goes unnoticed – this is a clumsy way of putting it – it remains in obscurity and all the investigator experiences is the connection with the dead person. What we see in the world of the spirit thus depends on what we intend to see. It is therefore understandable that the descriptions of the spiritual world may vary endlessly with different seers. Each one of them may have seen quite correctly what he was bound to see in view of the impulse which guided him when he had taken his soul and spirit out of the living physical body.

In this and the following lectures I shall describe what clairvoyant consciousness sees when it enters the world of the spirit with the intention of acquiring knowledge of the inner life of man, with its four spheres of perception, thinking, feeling and will, in order to discover what ebbs and flows in the human soul, causing it both joy and sorrow.

Let us suppose someone has developed clairvoyant consciousness to the point where the soul and spirit can be withdrawn from the living physical body in a way that normally only happens in the unconsciousness of sleep, and that this person performs the withdrawal with the express intention or impulse of acquiring knowledge, of being able actually to observe, the inner life of man. I am now going to try to describe what such an individual would experience.

The first experience of clairvoyant consciousness is that our world view undergoes a complete reversal. As long as we are in the body we look around us with the senses and think with our intellect. We see a world of mountains, rivers, clouds and stars, and at one point in this world we see ourselves as a minute entity in comparison with this great world. When clairvoyant consciousness begins to function outside the body, the whole situation is reversed. The world which ordinarily lies spread out before the senses and on which we reflect with the brain-bound intellect disappears from view and no longer gives rise to thought. Instead, we feel as if our very being were poured out into this world. If we have really come free of the body, the experience can be expressed in the following words: 'You are now poured out into the world at which you were merely looking until now; you are now in this world and up to a certain limit fill the whole space. You are actively moving in time.'

This is an experience to which we must first grow accustomed. Another way of describing it would be to say: 'What has been outside world is now inner world. It is not as if you now had this outside world inside you, but the feeling is that it has become inner world. You now live in the space in which things and events were spread out which you perceived with the senses and about which you had thoughts.' When clairvoyant consciousness is developed in a certain way, the tiny human being who was previously at the centre, with the horizon of the sense-perceptible world around him, now actually is our world. We look at it in the same way as we previously looked at the outside world which extended through space and progressed in time. We have become our own world.

Just think what a reversal of the human way of seeing the world it is when what we called 'I' before and which definitely was not the outside world, has now become the world outside, with everything tending towards it. It is as if from every point in space you were looking towards a single centre – and there see yourself. It is as if you were swimming forwards and backwards in time and at one particular point in one wave in the stream of time you find yourself. You have become your own world.

This is the first impression received when clairvoyant consciousness is used with the aim – again I emphasize this point – the express aim of acquiring knowledge of the inner life. It is strange: you go out of the body because you want to learn about the inner life and the first thing you meet is the human form itself. But how this form has changed! It is something which cannot be said often enough: If your intention, as you go out of the body, is to acquire knowledge of the inner life, then everything I am now going to tell you will happen, though of course it does not always have to be like this when people become clairvoyant.

How different the human form now appears! You know that you are looking at your own self. This is the you which you previously experienced from inside, in your skin and your blood. Now you are outside. To begin with you will only see the outer form, though it has been transformed. The eyes, or what used to be the eyes, shine like two suns; these are, however, inner suns, vibrant with light, sparkling and gleaming, with the sparkling light coming up and fading away again – suns which radiate light. This is how the eyes appear in the changed human form. The ears begin to sound, in a way; you will not see the ears which can be seen in the physical world, but you will feel that there is sound. The whole of the skin shines with a radiance which you are able to feel rather than actually see. In short, the human form appears to you as something which gives out light, sound, magnetic and electrical emissions and radiation.[1] These are clumsy expressions, however, and that is precisely because they are taken from the physical world.

When we first achieve clairvoyant experience, therefore, the world lying before us is the human being, radiant with light; the whole of the skin can be felt to be radiant, the eyes seen, the ears heard. We then know we have seen the physical body whilst outside the body and that this is how it presents itself from the vantage point of the spirit.

If we then try and become inwardly active whilst out there, outside the body, and enter into an activity which may be compared with reflection – it is different from ordinary thinking, for we are developing creative inner powers – we see something more in this radiant body; we see powers moving in it like a kind of circulating energy. And we then know that this is the life of thought seen from outside and that this life of thought is part of the ether body. We see the ether body as an actively moving thought life. It is like dark, circulating waves, a spiritual blood circulation. Dark waves give the body of light a strange appearance and force us to realize that we are now seeing from outside how the ether body is welling and boiling in the physical body.

Outside the body, therefore, we come to realize that there truly is a physical body and an ether body and we come to know what they look like when seen from outside.

It is possible to increase our inner powers even further. If only the things I have just described could be perceived, we would see ourselves as rather strange creatures in the world of the spirit. We would seem to be like creatures who are able to gain impressions of the outside world but are quite unable to feel anything inside. Yet something equivalent to feeling on the physical plane can also awaken when we are outside the body. It is not the kind of feeling we have when we are in the physical body but something equivalent to this. Previously the experience merely was: 'You are in space and move in the waves of time. You are in the space in which you previously saw people, creatures and events and you are in the flow of time in which you were perceiving with the senses.' When, however, the inner potential which is equivalent to feeling is awakened outside the body, the soul begins to grow into a knowledge that makes all kinds of things come to light out there, and we not only feel as if spread out through space, but perceive something which is in this space, something real that moves in the stream of time. We no longer see what we formerly saw by means of the body and its organs as we looked out on the world, but find ourselves in the inner reality of this outside world, in the spiritual reality that is alive and active in it. It is as if the space in which we formerly felt ourselves to exist was filled with countless stars, all in motion, and ourselves among them. We then know that we are experiencing ourselves in the astral body whilst outside the physical body, and that the world in which we merely felt ourselves to be has a content which now comes to life.

If we then look back at the radiant body with the dark thought-circulation of the ether body which we saw before, the physical body we have left behind appears different to us the moment we concentrate on the star life of the astral body. The difference may be expressed as follows: 'You are able to concentrate and look back on yourself and you see the radiant body and the ether body of thought. But when you are able to concentrate on yourself in such a way that a world of stars, which you know you fill completely, comes to life in you, and if you then look back to the physical body which you have left behind, the radiance and the circulation of thoughts may cease.' This is something which can be done at will, and the image which then arises is the image of our own true nature; it shows itself – there is no other way of putting it – as our personified karma. We human beings have something in us that is as if rolled up inside us and from which we create our particular destiny. Our destiny, our karma, now stands before us, and as we look at it we know: 'This is you, but it is you in your true inner moral nature, you yourself as you are in the world as an individual.'

And then another consciousness arises; this has something very oppressive about it. We see the whole of our personified destiny in such a way that we feel it to be intimately connected with our body and its earthly constitution. We come to the immediate realization that our muscles and the whole muscular system are a creation of this destiny of ours. And now comes the moment when we realize how different maya is from truth. As long as we are on the physical plane we believe that the muscular system consists of fleshy muscles, when in reality they are crystallized karma. Their composition, right down to the subtlest chemical level, is such that we carry our crystallized karma in our muscular system. It needs spiritual vision, however, to realize that when a person has, for example, used his muscles to proceed to a place where he then had a misfortune, this happened because there is an inherent spiritual power in his muscles which took him of its own accord to the place where he met with misfortune. The world order has crystallized our destiny in our muscular system, and in those muscles lives the spirit which in terms of the outer physical plane has crystallized, and without our conscious knowledge takes us to all the places where we must go, in accordance with our karma.

If we gain still more inner power and enter into further out-of-body experience of the inner life, something arises in us which in ordinary physical life is our will impulse. When the life of the will thus reveals itself we feel as if we were not merely in a stellar system, but in the sun of that stellar system. We feel at one with the sun of our individual planetary system. We might say that when we have inner experience of the astral body we know ourselves to be at one with our individual planetary system; when we experience ourselves outside the body with the ego, we know ourselves to be at one with the sun of our stellar system, with everything turning and tending towards this sun.

Looking back on ourselves when we are no longer inside but outside ourselves – anything that is outside us when we are in the physical body will be inside us when we are outside that body, and everything that is inside us when we are in the body will be outside when we are out of the body – something else presents itself. We realize why our body had to come into existence in the physical world and must in turn pass away. We become aware that spiritual powers and entities guide the growth and development of the human body and that others again destroy it. We also realize that our coming into being in, and passing away from, the physical world has crystallized in something quite specific, for we know it to be fundamentally connected with the skeletal system. When the skeletal system is built into the human physical body, the verdict is pronounced on the form in which human beings experience birth and death in the physical world. The way in which the skeletal system is crystallized and takes form in them determines the way in which they come into existence and pass away again. We realize that we could not be what we are in physical existence if the whole world had not joined forces to harden our physical nature to the point where it confronts us in the skeletal system. In this system – strange as it may seem – we come to revere the universal powers that rule the cosmos, powers which find their representation in all the spiritual entities concentrated in the life of the sun. We come to recognize the skeletal system as the ground plan of the human being with its outline traced in the world order, and we realize that our other physical organs are, in a way, suspended from it.

Clairvoyant vision of the inner world which has become outside world thus ends in a vision of the human skeleton seen from outside, which is the symbol of death. For in the final instance clairvoyance leads to the realization that the spiritual worlds have, as it were, created an external physical symbol for themselves;

we also realize that these are the worlds to which we truly belong in our inner being. We have entered these worlds by going out of the body, and this has shown us our true nature. Another thing we realize at this fourth stage is that when we act in the world, when we unfold our will, this is an inner power which acts unconsciously on the physical plane, a power we only come to know at this point. We now realize that when we take a single step forward, using the mechanics of the skeletal system, cosmic forces are involved in the process, and we only find ourselves truly in these forces when we experience our inner nature at this fourth stage outside the body.

Think of someone going for a walk, moving his limbs with the aid of skeletal mechanisms. The individual imagines he is doing this simply to suit himself. But it needed the whole world to provide the powers which enable us to use the mechanisms of the skeletal system for taking a walk, and the whole world had to be filled with the divine and spiritual forces which we only get to know when we have reached this fourth stage. The divine and spiritual cosmos lives in every step we take. We may think it is we ourselves who put one foot before the other, but we would not be able to do so if we did not live in the spiritual cosmos, the divine world.

As long as we are in our physical bodies we use our eyes to look all around us and we see the mineral world, the plant world, the animal world; we see mountains, rivers, oceans, lakes, clouds, sun, moon and stars. All these have an inner reality which we enter into only when we live outside the body in the way I have described. Then we know the spiritual essence that is hidden behind the radiant sun, the shining stars, behind mountains, rivers, oceans, lakes and clouds, and we know that it lives in the mechanics by which we move our bones. All this must be present.

We then also understand more clearly what we experienced at the third stage. Just as the will is closely connected with the skeletal mechanism, so are our feelings closely connected with the muscular system, which is a symbolical expression of the system of feelings. It needs the planetary system to build the kind of muscles we have, muscles which can be extended and contracted and in turn operate the mechanics of the skeletal system. We gain knowledge of the planetary system when we become conscious of being in the astral body. The whole planetary system lives in our muscles, just as the whole cosmos lives in the skeletal mechanics. The corresponding situation relating to our thoughts and sensory perceptions will be discussed in later lectures.

Spiritual insight reveals such things to us and we can see that it not merely gives us thoughts and ideas but becomes part of the whole of our inner life, so that we may truly know ourselves and become different people in the whole way in which we feel and think. If you accept the things that have been described as the experience of clairvoyant consciousness and let them come alive in your heart and mind, and if you then gather it all together ... how can we describe in a few short words the inner feeling for life that quickens in us when we know the results of clairvoyant investigation?

If we consider the way in which our absolutely ordinary, everyday moods and whims come to expression, the impression we gain is similar to the words spoken by Capesius and Benedictus at the beginning of my Mystery Play *The Soul's Probation*,[2] namely, that the goals the divine spirits set themselves and the thoughts they have thought through all the worlds come together in man. Summing this up in one vital feeling, we may say that we see human nature differently and know that the divine cosmos is to be found everywhere in it. Consciousness of this is quickened and waxes stronger, and having gained understanding in soul and heart we are able to say: Man can be understood only by recognizing that his whole being is born out of the divine and spiritual world.

When we perceive how feeling flows into the function of our muscles, how divine and spiritual cosmic forces flow into our bones, how the whole cosmos lives in the movements of our bones and the whole planetary system in the extension, contraction and relaxation of our muscles, and when we think this through and feel its reality, we can say with full understanding: Truly, man is born out of the divine world.

Ex deo nascimur
Out of God are we born.

LECTURE FOUR

The Vision of the Ideal Human Being

Vienna, 10 April 1914

YESTERDAY, WHEN WE SPOKE OF THINKING, feeling, will and perception, my task was to communicate certain experiences gained when in the course of spiritual investigation the human soul lives outside the body, with the purpose of learning something about the nature of the inner life. Today my task will be to present such experiences from another aspect, for it is only by observing the inner life from all kinds of different points of view that we can discover the real truth about it.

Try and really see in your mind's eye what I described yesterday, which is what the human soul sees when it is out of the body and looks back at the seer's own living body and everything which is connected with it physically, and what the soul experiences afterwards. Call back to mind the experiences of the astral body and the ego when they gain increasing strength in the space into which they enter when they leave the body. There is also another way of considering the matter. The point is that it needs genuine spiritual research to come to the riddles of existence, and fundamentally this is only possible if we look at the same thing from many different points of view.

Yesterday I described the point of view gained when the soul leaves the body by simply going out into space and beginning to live outside the body in space. Another way of going out of the body is the following. To find the way out of yourself, you first of all try to enter more deeply into yourself and link up with spiritual experiences through the element in the soul that is most akin to your memory. I have often said that we actually transform our inner life into something spiritual simply because as human souls were are able not only to perceive, think, feel and will, but also to store thoughts and perceptions in memory. In the public lecture given on 8 April I mentioned that the French philosopher Henri Bergson actually realized that the store of memories we hold cannot be regarded as directly connected with the body but must be taken as part of the inner life, something which is entirely soul and spirit by nature.[1]

And, in fact, when Imagination begins to develop in clairvoyant consciousness and the first impressions arise from the darkness of spiritual existence, the quality and the whole nature of these impressions are very similar to the store of memories we hold in the soul. When we begin to perceive with clairvoyant consciousness, the revelations from the spiritual world are like memory images, though infinitely more spiritual. We then become aware that our memory store is the first truly spiritual element in us, the first element through which we rise to some extent above the body. We also realize that we have to go further and draw on spiritual depths which are outside the experience we have of memory images in order to gain the floating images which belong to the realm of the spirit – like memory images but much more alive. This is something to hold onto: something arises from unfamiliar spiritual realms which lie beyond memory; our store of memories comes from experiences gained in the physical world.

If we now turn the inner eye back to everything we have experienced from the time in childhood when we perceived ourselves to be an 'I', that is, as far back as our memory will go, leaving aside anything external and thus living entirely in ourselves, so that we enter more and more deeply into our store of memories and recollect things of which we are not normally aware, we come closer and closer to the point in time which is as far back as memory will go. If we do this often so that we gain some practice in calling up long-forgotten memories – and this is possible – we strengthen our powers of recollection. A time will then come when images, or Imaginations, of things we did not know before, come up among our memories rather like flowers coming up among the grasses in a meadow. These come from entirely different depths of spirit than the memories which arise merely from the soul. And we then learn to distinguish between things that are in some way connected with our memories and the things that arise from spiritual foundations and spiritual depths. Gradually we are able to develop the power to let spiritual reality arise from its foundations.

This allows us to go out of the body in a different way from that described yesterday, where we went straight out of the body, as it were. By the method described today we first go back through our life. We enter deeply into our inner life and learn to strengthen the power of recollection until we are able to let spiritual realities arise among our memories. In the end this will enable us to penetrate beyond our birth, beyond conception and into the world of the spirit that was our home before we united with the hereditary substance for our present incarnation. Passing swiftly backwards through our life we find our way into the world of the spirit, into the time before we entered into this incarnation. There is a great difference between this method and the one described yesterday. Please take careful note of these differences, for in these lectures I am going to speak of many finer points and subtleties connected with life in the spirit. It is often difficult to find the right words for these, but it is possible to find the right approach and gain a reliable basis for our thinking if we become fully aware of these differences.

Leaving the body by the method I have just described is very different from the method I spoke of yesterday, where you feel that you are in a space that is outside the body. You leave the body and fill that space, as it were. If you follow the method given today, space ceases to have any meaning; you leave space and live entirely in time. In this case, it is meaningless to say 'I am out of the body', as those words suggest a position in space. What happens is that you feel yourself to be in a different time from your living body. You feel yourself to be in the 'before', in the time before your incarnation, and you perceive the body as existing afterwards. You are wholly in the flow and progress of time where 'before' and 'after' have taken the place of 'outside' and 'inside'.

Going out of the body in this way you are actually able to enter into the realms where we live between death and a new birth. You go back in time and come to know the life you lived before your present life on earth. Your life on earth presents itself in such a way that you ask: 'What lies ahead there in the future? What presents itself to me as the hereafter?' Here you have in more accurate detail what I have not been able to go into fully in the public lecture, which is, how we can actually enter into the realms where we live between death and a new birth.

This way of going out of the body has much greater inwardness than if one does so by the other method, which does not take us out of space. Anything connected with the truly inward depths of the soul can only be grasped if this second method is used. To begin with, let me tell you something that will show you how we must try and get behind the finer and more subtle aspects of human life.

We live our physical life here in a physical body. We use the senses, perceive the world, develop an idea of it, feel in it, and through our actions try to be of value in this world and be conscious of our actions. This is our everyday life on the physical plane. Yet every human being who wants to have real inner feeling for human dignity must know that there has to be a higher life, and indeed there has always been a higher life of the soul. There have always been religions which offered the realization of a higher life, and in future the science of the spirit will bring realization of a higher life. What are the goals of this higher life in which our thoughts, feelings and inner responses go beyond anything the physical plane has to offer? Some have only a dim idea of this in religious life, others see it clearly outlined in the science of the spirit, and it goes beyond anything the senses can perceive, that our brain-bound intellect is able to think and our bodies are able to accomplish in this world.

The human soul inclines toward life in the spirit. To be inwardly aware of the reality of such a life and know something about this life, which goes beyond physical life – this gives us our true worth. As long as human beings dwell in a physical body they seek to enhance their worth and gain an idea of their true destiny by sensing, seeking to gain a feeling for, and knowledge of, the world of the spirit. The keynote of religious life and anything connected with it should be: 'Look up to the spirit and feel that spiritual powers are active in the physical worlds.' And it will be the concern of those who consider the education of children to be a serious matter not to let children grow up in such a way that they live only with external and material ideas, but to convey to them ideas of another world.

Leaving aside the narrow and dogmatic elements which are to be found in religious systems, let us use the word 'religion' to denote something that draws human beings out of this physical world. With regard to the method I have just described, where the human soul goes beyond birth and conception into a world of the spirit which preceded life on earth, and is then also beyond space, let us ask: 'When we thus enter the world which lies between death and a new birth, do we find there anything which might be called a 'religion' of that spirit land, something which might be compared with religious life on earth?' Many details have already been given of the life between death and a new birth, and more will still have to be given. At the moment the question is, however: 'Is there anything like religion in that life of the spirit, something which may be said to relate to the experiences we gain in that life in the way the hints we get of the other world relate to everyday life on the physical plane?'

Someone who goes out of the body using the method I have described will find that there is something similar to a religious life in that spirit land. There you experience everything around you both spiritual entities and events in that world – in the same way as you experience physical entities and events in the physical world here on earth. The remarkable thing, however, is that all the time, or at least for the greater part of the time when you are in the life between death and a new birth, you have before you the image of the ideal human being – a tremendous spiritual figure. Here on earth, everything which goes beyond human nature is our religion. There, in the world of the spirit, the ideal human being is the religion. You come to understand that the different members of the spiritual hierarchies joined their intentions and powers so that man could gradually come into being in the stream of world evolution, as described in my book *Occult Science*. The gods had a vision of the ideal human being; the reality of this is not the physical human being as he is today, but a state of development where the life of the human soul and spirit reaches its highest level in a physical human being whose potential is fully realized.

Thus the gods have the image of man before them as their highest ideal, their religion. In their mind's eye they see, as if on the far shore of divine existence, the temple which is their supreme work of art, representing man as the image of divine being. When human beings are in the spirit land between death and a new birth, their further development consists in making themselves more and more ready to behold the temple which is the ideal of humanity. Here on earth, religious life is the exact opposite, for our inner feeling about it is that it must be a free decision, something we must find within ourselves, and that it also possible to deny the religious element if one is of a materialistic mind. The more we live on into the second half of the time between death and a new birth, the more clearly does the sublime ideal of humanity, the goal of the gods, present itself to the inner eye, so that we cannot possibly overlook it. Here on earth we may be irreligious because the soul loses sight of the spirit in the physical world; in the other world it is impossible to overlook the goal of the gods, for it stands out clearly. It is therefore particularly in the second half on life between death and a new birth that the image of the ideal human being presents itself as if on the shore of existence, that is to say, on the shore of onflowing time – please note that everything said at this point refers to time and is outside space. There can be no theory of religion in that world; instead, the essential substance of religion, which I have just described, is the subject of direct experience. No one can be irreligious in that world, for the religious ideal of spirit land stands before us. It is self-evident reality, the goal of the gods presented in the most powerful and glorious Imagination when we enter into the second half of our life between death and a new birth. We are then not able to develop a religion based on theoretical knowledge, but we nevertheless develop a kind of religion under the guidance of higher spiritual entities who are active on our behalf in that world.

We cannot be taught direct experience, or vision, during the second half of life between death and a new birth, for this comes of its own accord, but our will – feeling imbued with will, and will imbued with feeling – has to be quickened so that we may really strive towards the vision which lies before us. The will of gods and the feeling of gods flow into our will-imbued feeling and feeling-imbued will so that we may choose the path that leads to the goal. It is quite impossible to find the right words for a life which is so totally different, but perhaps we may say it like this: we 'receive instruction' in that life to help our understanding. Here on earth teachers have to go through ideas, mental images, if they are to influence our feeling. In the other world, when we have passed the halfway point between death and a new birth –

I have called this the 'midnight hour' in my last Mystery Play *The Soul's Awakening*,[2] and more will be said about it later – our will and feeling are not very much alive to the vision of the magnificent temple in the far distance of time. Then divine powers send glowing warmth through the inner powers of our soul. The kind of instruction we are then given speaks directly to our inmost being, so that we gradually gain the power and the will to take the path which leads to the ideal we see before us. In physical life we may be face to face with a teacher or instructor and yet feel that they are speaking to our heart from outside. When we are given instruction by our spiritual teachers who are members of the higher hierarchies we feel that they let their own powers flow directly into our inmost being. Earthly teachers speak to us; in the life between death and a new birth spiritual teachers pour their life into our souls as they give religious instruction in the spirit. More and more intensively we feel our teachers from the higher hierarchies to be within us and we feel ourselves to be more and more closely connected with them. As a result, our inner life gains in strength and power. 'You are more and more accepted by the gods, who live in you with ever increasing intensity and help you to gain in inner strength.' This is the essential feeling during life between death and a new birth, and particularly during the second half of it.

We see how everything in the other life is designed to make us gain immediate experience in the depths of the soul itself. But then we reach a very important point as we gain experience under the instruction of the gods between death and a new life. We see the ideal of humanity in the farthest distances of time, whilst the powers which our divine and spiritual teachers have given to us depend on what we have made of ourselves in the course of our incarnations and the human life we have lived before. And so, living onward from the cosmic midnight hour, which is exactly halfway between death and a new birth, moving onward in the stream of time and seeing the ideal of humanity in the far distance, we reach the point where we gain our final view of the ideal of humanity. Having reached this point we have to say to ourselves – of course we do not actually 'say' it, for it is an inner experience, but I have to use the words that belong to ordinary life: 'Divine and spiritual powers have been working on you and become more and more inward in your soul so that they now live in you. Now, however, you have reached the point where you can no longer take in these powers. You would have to be much more perfect than you are if you were to go on beyond this point.'

This is a moment of decision and we are faced with cruel temptation. The gods have done well for us, giving us everything they possibly can up to this point; they have made us as strong as the power we have gained so far in life will permit. This god-given strength is in us and now temptation comes, saying: 'You can now follow these gods; everything you are at this point can flow into the powers the gods have given you and you can enter into the worlds of the spirit. For the gods have given in great abundance.'

It would be possible for us to become entirely spiritual at this point; the prospect lies before us. But to do so we would have to turn aside from the path leading to the great human ideal. In other words, we would enter the worlds of the spirit taking all our imperfections with us. True, they would change into perfections there; they really would. We might enter with our imperfections and because we have been given divine powers we would have a real existence. Yet we would be entities who must renounce any potential still undeveloped in us, potential that could take us to the great human ideal. This would have to be renounced. Each time we are about to incarnate on earth again we are tempted to remain in the world of the spirit, enter into the spirit and develop what we already have, which is now filled with divine powers, renouncing any potential development towards the distant religious ideal of the divine and spiritual world. We are tempted to be irreligious in spirit land.

The temptation is all the greater because Lucifer's power over man is greatest at this moment in human evolution when he breathes the words: 'Seize the opportunity you now have; you can remain in the spirit; you can take everything you have developed into the light of the spirit.' Lucifer tries by all available means to make the soul forget the potential which still exists and the goal represented by the temple on the far shores of our existence in time.

The present state of humanity is such that we would not be able to withstand the temptation of Lucifer at this point if the spirits whom Lucifer opposes were not to take a hand in the affair. The gods who have their own avowed religion and guide the human being on the path to the human ideal, wage battle for the human soul with Lucifer. The outcome of the battle is that the archetypal image which the human soul has formed of earthly existence is cast out of time into space; existence in space is attracting it like a magnet. This is also the moment when the parents attract the soul like a magnet and the human being is transported into the spheres of space and gains a relationship to space. Because of this, everything around the human being which might be a temptation to remain in the world of the spirit is covered with a veil. Being enveloped in a physical body is an expression of this veiling. We are placed in a physical body so that we do not see what Lucifer desires to put before us. Once we are in the physical body and look at the world through our physical senses and the body-bound intellect, we lose sight of the aim we would seek to achieve in the world of the spirit when tempted by Lucifer. We then see the world of spiritual entities and events in the world of the spirit from the outside, in the way they show themselves to our senses and brain-bound intellect. And the spirits who guide us on the path to the ideal take charge of our development when we are in the physical body.

And now let us ask: How much goes on in the subconscious depths of our soul between birth and death without our knowing about it? If we had to achieve everything in full conscious awareness, we certainly would not be able to achieve existence on earth. In my book *The Spiritual Guidance of Man and Humanity*[3] I have shown that when human beings come to physical incarnation they must first of all mould the brain and nervous system and develop them further; they do it themselves but they do it unconsciously. All this is the expression of a far greater wisdom than anything human beings are able to grasp with their sense-bound intellect. Between birth and death a wisdom reigns in us which lies behind the world we perceive with the senses and think about with our brain-bound intellect. This wisdom which lies behind the world is hidden from us between birth and death. It moves and acts in subconscious depths of soul in us, where it has to take affairs in hand, as it were, because the human being must be snatched away for a time from a sight that would be a temptation. Under normal conditions of life, without careful training to take us into the world of the spirit, we would be tempted at every step, all the time we live in our physical bodies, to abandon all our undeveloped human potential and follow the upswing to the worlds of the spirit, taking our imperfections with us. We need our life on earth so that we may be out of reach of the temptation of Lucifer during this time.

Up to the point in time when we are taken into space, Lucifer has no power over us, for there is always still the opportunity for further development; Lucifer comes on the scene when we are on the point of decision. Because of our previous life, we are unable to progress and so we are tempted to go astray and remain in the world of the spirit, keeping our imperfections. The progressive gods whom Lucifer opposes protect us by snatching us away from the world of the spirit, hiding it from us, and doing the things that have to be done out of the world of the spirit which lies behind our conscious awareness.

And so we stand here in the world as human beings, conscious in our physical body, and say to the gods: 'Thanks be to you, for you have left us just as much possibility of knowing something of the world as is good for us.' If we were to see behind the threshold at the horizon of our conscious awareness, every moment would put us in danger of not wishing to achieve the goal of humanity. Between death and rebirth we were in the brighter, higher state of consciousness in which we are in the spirit, with spiritual worlds and spiritual entities all around us. We had to be taken out of that state and into the world of space where we are unable to see the world that we are not strong enough to bear until we have gone through the time between birth and death. During this time, when we have been snatched from the world of the spirit so that we are surrounded by material things and not by the world of the spirit, we have been given new impetus towards the far distant goal of ideal humanity. All the time we are on earth, when the conscious mind does not perceive the world of the spirit, the divine spirits who impel us forward are at work in us; here their work is not disturbed by our consciousness nor by our being tempted to follow Lucifer. The divine spirits infuse the strength into us which we shall need if after going through the gate of death we are to press forward again and come a little closer to the ideal of humanity.

With these words I have indicated a further mystery which lies behind human existence. And I think it is good at Eastertide to turn our hearts and minds to the conditions of life between death and rebirth which are to be to be found by going out of the body by the inward path, and to the life which follows when we are in a physical body. We turn to life between death and rebirth and become aware of the guidance given by the good divine spirits to help us on our way forward. We look up to them as to our past life in the spirit, and we now understand that our present life in a body between birth and death has been given to us by the gods in order that they may take care of our further development for a while, when there is no need for ourselves to take an active part. We perceive the world, think in the world, feel in it, will in it, we store up memories which allow us to have continuity in life, and all the time divine spirits are at work behind this conscious life. They continue to guide the stream of time, having released us into space. There we have just as much conscious awareness as the gods consider it right for us to have, whilst it is their will to continue to work behind this consciousness and guide our destinies towards the great ideal of humanity, which is the ideal of their religion.

Looking at our inner life in this way – it is the inner life which our conscious mind is unable to perceive and explore under normal conditions of life – let us try and enter wholly into the feeling: 'Here something lives in you which you cannot fathom with the normal powers of human life; yet it is the deepest and inmost life of the soul.' Let us try to become aware of this life of soul so deeply hidden inside us and then try to become aware that the gods reign in this life of the soul which we ourselves do not guide. This will give us the right feeling, a true Easter feeling, for the god who reigns in us. It is to this end that I wanted to say these things today and not so much for their abstract content.

If the soul is able to contemplate what is revealed to it as it goes out of itself into space and fills space and is able to know: 'Out of the divine I am born,' what I have said today will deepen that knowledge, so that the soul may be aware: 'With everything I know and everything accessible to my soul in perception, thinking, feeling and will, I am born out of a deeper soul life which is still with the gods, moving in the stream of time, but moving together with the divine principle.' We become aware of a knowledge which can come to expression in a much deeper sense than the sense in which I spoke at the end of yesterday's lecture. As the result of today's studies, the words, 'Out of God we are born' can be spoken with much deeper meaning, for we realize that this soul and everything it is able to know about itself is at every point in time born out of the divine, and at every point in time we can fill our deepest, inmost being with these words:

>Out of God we are born.
>*Ex deo nascimur.*

LECTURE FIVE

The Senses and the Luciferic Temptation

Vienna, 11 April 1914

IN TODAY'S LECTURE, ATTENTION WILL BE DRAWN to a number of definite results of occult investigation which are eminently fitted to show us the true nature of the human being, but will also show us how complex the human being really is. Can we think otherwise, when we reflect that the true image of man, the ideal of what human beings can be if they develop all the qualities and faculties within them, is fundamentally the religion of the gods, and that all the spirits of the different hierarchies, whose connection with the true nature of human beings we can come to know, work towards a common goal, with the object of building the human being out of the whole cosmos as the very purpose and meaning of this cosmos?

The first thing to be said is that the sensory perceptions we have of the world around us – as they appear to the conscious mind – actually are only a small part of all the things that surge towards us. We are in the physical world, with our sense organs opened, contemplating the world with our brain- and nerve-bound intellect and trying to explain it to ourselves. Yet only a small part of everything that surges towards us actually becomes an idea in our conscious mind. Light, colours, sounds and so on, are infinitely richer in content that we are able to realize. Modern physicists merely take a childlike view of the world when they say that colours, light, and so on, are based on physical, substantial processes such as the oscillations of atoms. It really is a childlike way of looking at things, for in reality the following happens.

Sensory perception must be investigated with the eye of clairvoyance, for it is only by thus observing the actual process of sensory perception that we can understand how human beings relate to the world around them, even if we do not go beyond the physical plane. Suppose something produces an effect on our eyes: we perceive light or colour, and so become conscious of the sensation of light or colour. The remarkable discovery made in the course of spiritual investigation is that something else also appears in the human being. When we perceive light or colour, a kind of corpse of the light or the colour appears in us at the same time as the sensation of the light or colour itself. The eye causes us to have the inner experience of light or colour. The light streams towards us and brings about the experience of light, but when we look more deeply, we discover that while we have the light in our consciousness, something which is present everywhere in our very being must die in order that we may experience the light. We cannot gain a perception, or sensation, of anything outside ourselves unless something of a corpse-producing process filters through the sensation that arises rather like a consequence of it.

Someone who is doing spiritual investigation has to say: I am looking at a person and I know he s experiencing the colour red. I also see that the red which is in his conscious mind lets something pour our over the whole person and fill his whole being — in so far as it has entered into his skin and within the boundaries of his ether body — with something like the corpse of that colour, and kills something in him. Just think of it: when we face the physical world and our sense organs are open, we are also always taking in the corpses of our sensory perceptions. These are like phantoms, but active phantoms. Whenever we perceive the outside world with the senses, something dies in us. This is a remarkable phenomenon. And the spiritual investigator must ask himself: What is really happening here? What is the cause of this remarkable phenomenon?

We have to consider the true nature of the light that surges towards us. There are many things behind it, and the light itself is merely the advance guard. One thing which is not behind it is the wave motion which is the product of the imagination of physicists. Behind the light and everything we perceive with the senses is in the first place something we can only understand if we use spiritual science and see the world with the aid of Imaginations, creative images. If we were able to see and perceive everything which lives in the light, or in sound, or heat, we would perceive the creative Imagination which lies behind the things that reach our consciousness. Within this, Inspiration would reveal itself, and within Inspiration, Intuition. The things which reach the conscious mind may be regarded as the top layer, the froth on whatever it is that is winging towards us. In it lives what could become Imagination, Inspiration and Intuition in us if it were to come to consciousness.

Sensory perception therefore gives us only a quarter of everything that surges towards us; the other three quarters enter into us without coming to awareness. When we are experiencing a colour, the creative Imagination, the Inspiration and the Intuition belonging to it enter into us; it is as if they were pushing down into us through the surface of the colour experience. If we take a closer look at these last three invaders, we find that if they were really to enter into the human organism in the way they want to, they would cause us to become spiritual whilst we are still in physical existence between birth and death here on earth. I spoke of this spiritualizing process yesterday, saying that it was a possible result of Lucifer's temptation. The effect of this Imagination, Inspiration and Intuition would be that we develop the urge to leave aside all the potential capacities we have which might help us to work towards the ideal human being of the far distant future. Instead, we would want to become spiritual here and now, with everything we are. We would want to be spiritual at the level of perfection we have now reached through previous existence. So we would say to ourselves: It is too much of an effort to become truly human, for the path that will take us to the future is difficult. Let us ignore our human potential. We prefer to become angels, with all our present imperfections, for this will make us spiritual and take us straight into the world of the spirit. It will mean, of course, that we shall be less perfect than we could be in the cosmos, seeing that we have the potential to be perfect, but we shall be spiritual, angelic beings.

Here again you see the importance of what is called 'the threshold to the world of the spirit' and the spirit who is known as 'the Guardian of the Threshold'. The Guardian stands at the point of which I have just spoken. He allows only the sensory experience to come to our conscious awareness, keeping out the Imagination, Inspiration and Intuition that would immediately make us want to become spiritual, just as we are, forgoing all further life as human beings. Imagination, Inspiration and Intuition have to be veiled from us, the door of our consciousness closed against them. They do, however, enter into our essential nature, and as they do so, without being illuminated in the light of the conscious mind, and we are obliged to let them descend into the dark depths of the subconscious, the spiritual entities of whom Lucifer is the opponent enter into us from the other side, and battle then commences in us between Lucifer, who sends his Imagination, Inspiration and Intuition into us, and these other spirits. We would behold this battle taking place whenever we perceive anything with the senses, but it is hidden from us – though not from clairvoyant vision – by the threshold that has been set.

You will now realize that a great deal is actually going on in the inner depths of the human being. The outcome of the battle taking place in us is a kind of corpse, a partial corpse. It represents something in us which must become entirely material, like a mineral deposit, so that we shall not be able to make it spiritual. If the battle between Lucifer and his opponents did not produce this corpse, we would have the outcome of Imagination, Inspiration and Intuition in us and would rise directly into the world of the spirit. The corpse weighs us down; it is the means by which the good spirits – Lucifer's opponents – keep us in the physical world for the time being. They keep a veil over the otherwise inevitable urge to be spiritual, so that we may work towards the ideal human being, seeking to develop all our potential qualities. It is because we have this deposit, this corpse-like phantom developing in us each time we perceive anything with the senses, that we kill the urge to be spiritual which is constantly arising in us. Something arises in us when the deposit is formed. It is something I have mentioned before, and it is important that we understand it in all its implications.

When you look into a mirror, you have a pane of glass before you, and you would see right through this if it had not been silvered. The silvering makes the glass reflect anything in front of the mirror. If you were to come face to face with your physical body in such a way that you experienced not only the sensory perceptions entering into it, but also the Imaginations, Inspirations and Intuitions, you would be looking right through your physical body. The feeling would be such that you would say something like this to yourself: 'I do not want to have anything to do with this physical body; I shall ignore it and rise into the spiritual world just as I am.' Yes, your physical body would present itself to you just like a pane of glass which has not been silvered. As it is, the physical body has the corpse within it, just like the silvered backing of a mirror. Everything is reflected in it, but only to the extent to which we have 5perceived it with the senses. The corpse which is always in us is like a mirror-coating given to the whole body, and because of this we see ourselves in the physical world. It is this which makes us individual physical entities in the physical world. Here you see the complexity of the human being.

Let us take the other case, where we do not merely perceive but also think. When we think, it is not a matter of sensory perceptions. Thoughts may be triggered by sensory perceptions, but thinking as such is a more inward process. When we are thinking, we do not make an impression on the physical body, but certainly on the ether body. Yet here, too, not everything contained in our thoughts enters into us. If it did, we would feel living, elemental beings pulsing in us every time we think; we would feel as if we were teeming with life inside. I once said, in Munich, that if we were to experience thoughts as they really are, we would feel ourselves to be in a maze of activity, rather like an ant heap; everything would be alive.[1] We are not aware of this life in our human thinking, because again it is only the froth that reaches the conscious mind, creating shadowy images of the thoughts that come up in our thinking. On the other hand, the vital powers that are alive in our thoughts go down into the ether body. We do not consciously perceive the elemental spirits flitting through us; all we perceive is an extract of these, something like the shadow they cast. The other part, the life of the thoughts, enters into us. The result is that a battle again arises, this time between the progressive spirits and Ahriman, or the ahrimanic spirits. The outcome of the battle is that the thoughts do not act in us as they would if they were living entities. If they did, we would feel ourselves to be inside the life of the thought entities as they move hither and thither. Instead, our etheric body, which otherwise would be completely transparent, is made non-transparent, as it were; I would say something like a smoky quartz or cairngorm, with dark layers in it. Quartz as such is quite transparent and pure. This is how darkness of spirit fills our etheric body, and this is our store of memories.

The store of memories arises when the above-mentioned processes cause thoughts to be reflected, as it were, in the etheric body, but now in time, going as far back as our memory extends in physical life. Our memory therefore holds thoughts which are reflected out of time. Deep down in the ether body, the good divine spirits who are opposed by Ahriman are at work, skilfully combining the powers which will give new life to the elements which died in the physical body as the result of the abovementioned processes. A corpse has to be produced in the physical body to prevent us from following the urge to become spiritual even though we are far from perfect. At the same time the ether body provides the power to rekindle life. The elements which were killed can thus be given new life and form in future.

We now see for the first time the significance of 'before' and 'after'. If we were to let the Imaginations, Inspirations and Intuitions which enter into us take full effect right here and now, we would be following Lucifer[2] and would become spiritual. But because they are cast into the future, and do not take effect now, but are preserved as seeds for the future, they regain their true nature. At the present time, we should misuse these elements; in future, however, when we have gone through the gate of death, we shall use them to shape a new life for ourselves out of the world of the spirit. Used in the physical world, these powers would induce us to become spiritual with all our imperfections. After death they induce us to return to life on earth again. Things therefore work in opposite ways in the different worlds.

Having considered our thinking, let us now consider our feeling. Again, any feeling response in us falls short of what it could be according to its full inner potential. Feelings of which we are conscious are mere shadow images of what really lives in us, for our feelings, too, have spiritual reality. Remembering what I said in the first lecture, you will realize that the spiritual entities who are behind the whole of our planetary system live in our feelings; it is merely that we have no conscious awareness of this. Our feelings as we know them are within our range of consciousness; the rest stays outside. What does this really mean? It is extremely difficult to put these things in the words of our everyday language. We have said that sensory perception and thinking give rise to a 'killing' process in us, though in the case of thinking there is also the counter-effect in which something is kindled that will be alive in the future. We also have to say that every feeling we have or develop does not fully come to birth or into existence. If everything we have in us when we feel were to emerge, the spirit which lives in the feeling would take hold of us and fill us with energy in quite a different way. However, the element which lies behind the feeling, making it into a living entity whose life is fed out of the whole planetary system, does not emerge as such. The feeling, too, emerges only as a shadow of its real self. The result is that whenever we enter into the world of our feelings with a deep sense of our humanity, we actually have a sense of dissatisfaction with every one of our feelings. We feel every one of them could be more intense and stand out more clearly. It is particularly with regard to our feelings that our hearts must really tell us: Our feelings could tell us much more than they actually do; they are hiding part of our inner life, something deep down in the soul that is only half born.

The same holds true, but even more so, with regard to the will – everything we may want or desire. Behind the will is the spiritual ground of all being, whose true dwelling place is the sun. In the will lives not only the principle which lives in the planets but the principle which lives in the whole of the sun. It is hidden, however. Our will is even less fully born than our feeling. We would be filled with it in a very different way indeed, if everything it contains really came to conscious awareness. Only the uppermost froth, utterly superficial, comes to expression; the rest is hidden from us. The question is, why is a whole world of things hidden from us in feeling and will? The reason is that we would not be able to bear it if we were to see them from the physical plane. They would present themselves as something we would want to ward off, turning away from them.

The element which remains unborn in our feeling and in the will is our evolving karma. Let us say we feel hostile towards someone – to give a concrete example. The hostile feeling which comes to conscious awareness is merely the ripple on the surface; powers which extend over the whole of the planetary system are contained in this feeling. Yet it is precisely the hidden part which says to us: With your hostile feeling you are letting something imperfect take root in you; this must be balanced out. If the element which lives deep down in us were to emerge, we would immediately have before us the Imagination of the karmic element which must balance out the hostile feeling. And because we would be judging this from the standpoint of the physical plane, we would join forces with Lucifer and Ahriman to avoid the balancing-out process. It is, however, hidden from us when we are on the physical plane. The Guardian of the Threshold hides it from us for the simple reason that on the physical plane we cannot judge the part of our feelings and will impulses which remains unborn; we can do so only when we are in the world of the spirit between death and a new birth. Then we actually desire things we would otherwise never desire and we want to see anything by way of a hostile attitude balanced out. For when we are there we take a genuine interest in the religion of the gods, which is the ideal of humanity which wants to make us into perfect human beings. This tells us that anything caused by hostile feelings must be balanced out by applying the opposite. The unborn part of our feelings and will impulses must be preserved and should only emerge at a future time, after death.

I have now presented to you four elements from the inner core of the human soul. The unborn part of our feelings lives in the astral body, the unborn part of our will in the ego. When we perceive the world around us we have a kind of physical phantom corpse in us which is really the mirror-backing for the physical body. And we have an element of darkness in the ether body. Our astral body holds something which does not come to birth between birth and death, and part of the will also does not come to birth. These four elements in us have to be kept for the time between death and a new birth. Yet they live in us as the core of our soul just as surely as the seed for the next year lives in a plant. You see that we can are not only able to speak of a core of the soul as such, but also to understand its four elements. If an inner feeling gives rise to disquiet, let us say, and if we are not really satisfied with our life, this is due to pressure that the unborn part of our feelings exerts on the part which has come to consciousness. How can we avoid this pressure? The pressure, you see, is a constant threat to human beings, for it creates disharmony in us with regard to our feelings and our will, which in the sense of the first lecture (9 April) are the inner life. If there was genuine harmony between the parts of feeling and will that have been born and the parts that remain behind the threshold of consciousness, we would be happy and contented people in this physical world. This is where the reason for all inner dissatisfaction is to be found, for all our inner dissatisfaction is due to pressure from the subconscious parts of our feeling and will.

I have to add that the essential nature of human beings has changed in this respect in the course of evolution. Today, things are exactly the way I have described, but they have not always been like this. In earlier times of human evolution, let us say during the ancient Persian, Egyptian and Indian epochs, sensory perceptions were received in exactly the same way. But the Imaginations, Inspirations and Intuitions they contained were not quite as ineffective as they are today. They did not kill the inner physical life as completely as they do now, nor did they provide such dense mineral deposits. The reason was that when sensory perceptions streamed in from the outside, something would spring up from the other side, under certain conditions, out of feeling and will. If we were to go back to the earlier times of the ancient Egyptian or Babylonian civilizations, for example, and observe the human beings who lived then, we would find their sensory perceptions to have been of quite a different nature. They came face to face with the physical world just as we do, but their bodies were still organized in such a way that the Imaginations hidden in their sensory perceptions were not as deadly in their effect, but came to people with some degree of life in them. Being alive, they called forth the counter-image of the element which today is completely hidden in the ego and the astral body. The spiritual entities of the sun principle and the planetary system pushed against the sensory perceptions from inside and, as it were, mirrored the element brought to life through the Imagination. For the people of the ancient Egyptian and Babylonian civilizations, there were times when they looked at the physical world around them and took in not only the physical perceptions we gain today, but perceptions which came alive. They would know there was something behind their sensory perceptions which came into its own in Imaginations. They were therefore not so foolish as to suppose, the way our modern physicists do, that there were oscillating atoms behind the things they perceived. They knew there was life behind them. And so images of the starry heavens full of life and even images of the sun would arise in them, radiating outward in response. This was particularly so during the ancient Persian civilization, when something of the inner spiritual power of the sun would shine out in them when they perceived the outside world – and this was Ahura Mazda.

Going back to still earlier times, we find this meeting between the inner and the outer to have been even stronger. Today it can no longer be so, but there can be a substitute, and here we come to a point where the very nature of the matter can help us to gain a true understanding of the task we have been set in the context of the anthroposophical view of life.

A substitute must be created. We relate to the world around us through our sensory perceptions. We think about these, but the part of them which is not accessible to us has a deadening effect and fills us with darkness. We can, however, bring life into this through anthroposophy. It is precisely by this means that we develop the kind of science which is presented in the evolution of Saturn, Sun and Moon evolution in my *Occult Science*. Every human being has knowledge of this process of evolution, but only deep down at a subconscious level. If they were able to see this without the necessary preparation, people would not want to be human beings on earth. They would feel that the Earth was no concern of theirs and would wish that human evolution had come to an end with the Moon evolution. Everything we are able to discover through the science of the spirit throws light on the hidden aspects of past evolution when it enters into us, for when we are able to see through the veil of our sensory perceptions, we find that essentially the Imaginations, Inspirations and Intuitions which are alive in those perceptions but do not enter into us, relate to the past that lies behind us.

It is not quite the same in regard to what lives in our feeling and in our will. People may say – and many people feel compelled to do so today: 'Why should I care about anything those cranks are thinking up concerning a supersensible world? I refuse to accept such ideas.' People who say this have no notion of why religions have developed in world evolution. One thing all religious ideas have in common is that they relate to things which cannot be perceived with the senses. Human beings need religious ideas to meet an inner need, for ideas derived from anything we are able to perceive with the senses will never give our feeling and will the impulse which will give us impetus power after death. The ideas we have gained through sensory perceptions and the brain-bound intellect will be of no use to us when it comes to giving effective power to the part of our feeling and will which does not come to birth during life. The impulse and impetus we shall need after death can only come from ideas that do not relate to outward reality but make us turn to higher things and look up to a world of the spirit. Religious thinking is to think of things which cannot be active in us now but will be active after death. When we take in religious ideas, these are not merely ideas based on knowledge but something which will be active after death –

which means that now, when we are in a physical body, people who refuse to give any thought to active principles of this kind will laugh about them and, being materialists, reject them. But if they do not let ideas of the supersensible enter into them, their power to bring the unborn elements in their feeling and will to development will be crippled.

This is why I have to stress over and over again that clairvoyant consciousness throws light on the past. This is recognized again today, as are the Imaginations, Inspirations and Intuitions which are veiled by the world perceptible to the senses and have an influence on that world. In earlier times, this was given to human beings as religious faith and belief, in order that they might not lose all impetus for the time after death and might have something in the inner core of the soul that would keep them alive once they had laid aside their physical bodies. Now the time has come when people should develop ideas on the worlds of the spirit, which is possible, thanks to the science of the spirit. It therefore cannot be stressed often enough that whilst one needs to be a spiritual investigator to discover these things in the world of the spirit, we all have a secret language deep down in our souls which enables us to understand what spiritual investigators have discovered and make known to us. It is sheer prejudice of the intellect and the senses which makes people consider the ideas relating to the supersensible world which are presented by spiritual investigators to be nonsense and figments of the imagination. If we accept these ideas they will give impetus to the inner core of our being, so that in all future ages it will find its way in the cosmos. Investigation of the contents of the spiritual world is only possible if one has achieved esoteric development; but to have knowledge of these contents, to work through them inwardly in consciousness and have ideas and concepts of them, to make them our own and know for certain that the soul exists in the world of the spirit – this is something human beings will need more and more as essential nourishment for soul and spirit.

We see, therefore, how the mission of our anthroposophical movement can be understood out of the reality of the situation. In earlier times, human understanding was given life from above, with the contents for this coming from below. The ancients therefore had immediate awareness, but this gradually became dull and obscured. If this had not happened, human beings would not have achieved full ego consciousness, for they can only do so by developing the phantom corpse in the living physical body of which I have spoken. Being transparent, the physical body must, as it were, be coated like a mirror, and only when the coating is complete are we able to say: I am an 'I'. The complete coating only developed slowly and gradually in the course of human evolution. It had reached completion at the time of the Mystery of Golgotha. Before then, elements from above and below still came together in the human being. Both were completely forced out when the mirror was fully coated and human beings perceived everything as mirrored by the physical body.

What did actually happen at that time? Let us take a close look at this. Picture to yourselves the conscious awareness of people who lived before the Mystery of Golgotha. The life-giving quality of Imaginations came from outside, and images of the world of the spirit outside the human being arose from inside. We know people were able to let such images rise up in those times when in a reduced state of consciousness. Initiates who at that time were able to see the living encounter in the soul between life-filled Imaginations coming from outside and visions arising from inside would not say: 'Human beings are perceiving these things on their own', but rather: 'Jahve, or Jehovah – this would be in the case of the ancient Jews – is inside the human being and looking at his world. The god is thinking in the human being.' Today, in our present cycle of evolution, we say: 'I think.' Those who knew of these things in earlier times would say: 'The gods think in us' when visions came from the world of the spirit. Those who recognized the one god who represented the unity of the divine world would say: 'Jahve thinks in human beings, who are the stage for the divine thoughts.' People knew themselves to be filled with these thoughts and therefore said: 'The gods think in me.'

Human evolution demanded, however, that this became increasingly less possible. We might say that increasing darkness met the visions and thoughts of the gods in the human being as the phantom corpse gained in strength and importance. A time was approaching when thoughts would no longer come from human beings to meet the gods. The divine entity who may be said to have been thinking through the human being felt that its consciousness, which consisted in its thoughts, was growing dull and fading away. A longing then arose in this divine entity to awaken to life a new form of consciousness. Human beings merely come to a different form of consciousness. The gods create something essential to themselves when they create a new consciousness. Christ was the essential principle to arise for the divine entity of which we are speaking when it felt its consciousness fading. Christ is the child of the divine entity and Christ restores consciousness of divine nature in human life and activity. And so the essence of Christ had to become part of essential human nature.

We have to realize that when we perceive the world through the senses we continually let a process of dying flow into us; when we think about this world we let darkness and obscurity flow in, and with our feelings and will impulses we let elements flow into us which are unborn. We let our dying and those unborn elements in us which we will only be able to use when we are dead, flow into the subconscious depths of our being. It would all be feeble and crippled if we were unable to let it flow into the Christ essence which the divine entity brought to birth for itself as the essence of a new consciousness.

Awareness of this can come when, in the light of spiritual science, we perceive the true meaning of the whole of evolution, which is: We send the elements of dying which are in us down into subconscious depths, where they are received by Christ, who lives as he comes to meet us. Christ comes to live in the element which dies in us, grows dark and remains unborn. We let the things that must die go down into death in us so that we may come close to the true ideal human being with everything we are. But we pour the dying which is in us into the Christ essence which has been part of human evolution since the founding of Christianity. We know that the elements of feeling and will which remain unborn in us are received into the Christ substance into which they sink down after death.

There – within us – Christ has been living since he went through the Mystery of Golgotha. We let the dying that comes with all sensory perception go down into Christ. We let the darkening of our thinking go down into Christ, sending our darkened thoughts into the light of the Christ Sun. And when we go through the gate of death, our unborn feeling and will impulses enter into the Christ substance. When we gain real understanding of evolution, we say:

                We die into Christ.
                In Christo morimur.

LECTURE SIX

Wisdom in the Spiritual World

Vienna, 12 April 1914

IN THE PUBLIC LECTURE WHICH I GAVE on 8 April, I tried as far as it is possible in such a lecture to give a broad outline of human life between death and rebirth. This will be considered in greater depth in the next two lectures, so that it will also shed more and more light on life in the physical world. If we are to go into this more deeply, however, we need the preparation which was given in the first three lectures and will also be given today.

Speaking to our friends in one place or another, I have often said that if we want to get to know and understand the worlds of the spirit in which we live between death and rebirth, we must gradually acquire concepts and ideas which simply cannot be acquired through experiences and insights gained on the physical plane, but which will become increasingly more important to us, particularly also for our life on the physical plane. Let us begin by making clear distinction between experience in the world of the spirit and experience on the physical plane. This must inevitably seem strange and may quite take us aback when we hear it for the first time, making us think that these things are hard to understand. But the more we come to be at home in the science of the spirit, the more we shall find them easier and easier to understand.

When we go through the physical plane and let the experiences we gain there live in us, one thing must really strike us, if we think about it, and this is that the physical plane offers what we call 'reality'. We might say that the less people are spiritual, the more they base themselves on the reality which is so much in evidence on the physical plane. The situation is different when it comes to acquiring insight and understanding of reality. As children we have to be trained to develop the abilities which enable us to acquire insight and understanding of the physical plane, and we have to go on working at this. It needs mental effort to acquire insight. The physical world, that is, outer reality, does not freely yield up the wisdom and the laws which lie hidden in it. We have to acquire insight into the wisdom and the laws. Human efforts to gain knowledge actually consist in actively gaining access to the wisdom and the laws which are inherent in everything we learn from passive experience.

The situation is entirely different when we enter into the world of the spirit, which we do either by going through the training which will make us spiritual investigators, or by going through the gate of death. Please note that the relationship which individuals have to their spiritual environment is not always the same as the one I am going to describe; but it is like this in important moments and with important experiences. In life on the physical plane, too, we do not always toil after knowledge; we take a break from this work as from any other work. The things I am going to describe are not a constant necessity in the world of the spirit, but they are required at times.

Surprisingly, human beings do not lack wisdom in the world of the spirit. We may be fools in the physical world and yet have wisdom simply come to us in all its reality when we are in the world of the spirit. Things we have to work hard to acquire, labouring day after day if we want to have them, are ours in the world of the spirit just as nature is ours all around us in the physical world. They are always there in great abundance. In a way it would be fair to say that the less wisdom we have acquired on the physical plane, the more abundantly will wisdom come to us on the spiritual plane. We do, however, have a definite task to perform with regard to the wisdom of the spiritual plane.

Lecture Six 107

During the last few days I have spoken of the fact that on the spiritual plane we have the ideal human being before us who is the religion of the gods, and that we must work our way towards this. We are unable to do so unless we are able to apply our will – will combined with feeling, or feeling combined with will – in such a way that we are always taking something away from that wisdom, reducing it and causing it to darken. Here, on the physical plane, we have to grow in wisdom; there we must reduce wisdom, for the less we are able to take away from it, the less we find the powers which enable us to gain the powers we need if we are to come close to the ideal of humanity in our true being. The wisdom we take away we are able to transform inside ourselves, making it into the vital powers which impel us towards the ideal of humanity. We have to gain those vital powers by transforming the abundant wisdom which flows towards us between death and rebirth, for this alone enables us to move towards our new incarnation in the right way. When we return to earth we must have taken so much of that wisdom and transformed it into vital powers that we are able to penetrate the hereditary substance provided by our parents with enough vital powers to organize it.

When you meet an out-and-out materialist after death, someone who would not accept the reality of the spirit at all when on the physical plane, and who all his life would have been saying: 'The things you are saying about the spirit are utter foolishness and your wisdom is simply the figment of your imagination; I refuse to accept any of it; as far as I am concerned only the description of physical nature actually counts', you will see so much wisdom flowing towards this individual from all directions that he will be positively overcome. To the extent to which he did not believe in the spirit when here on earth, he is surrounded by wisdom over there. His task is to take this wisdom and transform it into vital powers which will enable him to create a physical reality in his next incarnation. The wisdom will not allow itself to be taken, however; it stays as it is and he cannot make it into reality. The horrendous punishment he faces is that whilst in his last life on the physical plane he based himself only on reality, utterly denying the spirit, he now cannot escape the spirit and is unable to bring it to realization. The danger he faces is that he will not even be able to return to the physical world with powers created by himself. All the time he will be living in fear of being pushed into the physical world by the spirit and into an existence which denies everything he considered right in his previous life, and he would be unable to achieve reality by himself.

Surprising as this may seem, it is the truth. To be an out-and-out materialist and deny the spirit before death is the best way to drown in the spirit after death and be unable to find the kind of reality which alone meant something before death. The individual then is smothered, or drowned, in the spirit.

We have to acquire these ideas more and more fully as we study spiritual science. If we do this, they will also take us through physical life in a harmonious way, showing us how the two sides of life have to supplement and balance each other. They lay the foundations for the instinct which will help us to create this balance in the way in which we conduct our life.

Let me give you another instance of the connection which exists between the physical life and life in the spirit. Let us take a single, concrete case, and assume we have lied to someone here on the physical plane. Please note, I am referring to a particular instance. If we have lied to someone, this would be at a particular point in time. The corresponding event in the world of the spirit will also be at a particular point in time. A time will come when we are in the world of the spirit, through initiation or through death, when the soul is entirely filled with the truth we should have spoken. It then torments us to the same extent as we deviated from it when we uttered the lie. All you have to do, therefore, is to lie on the physical plane, and a time will come in the world of the spirit when you are tormented by the truth, which lives and burns in you so that you cannot bear it. We suffer because we then see: this is the truth. We are not in a condition, however, to gain pleasure from this truth. To be tormented by good things, knowing full well that they should uplift you – this is a peculiar quality of the experiences you have in the world of the spirit.

You only need to have been lazy with regard to something where you should have been hard at work and a time will come in the world of the spirit when the eagerness to work which you did not have when it was needed comes alive in you. There will be a time when we experience an inner necessity and feel we simply must put this eagerness into effect inside us. We give ourselves up to it entirely and know it to be something of immense value, but it torments us and we suffer.

Another instance concerns something where we do not have much choice, perhaps, because it has to do with things that happen more beneath the surface in life. Let us assume we have had an illness in life which has caused pain, or the like. At some point in time when we are in the world of the spirit we will experience the opposite mood or state of mind, feeling ourselves to be in health. This mood of being in health will strengthen us to the same extent to which the illness weakened us before.

Now, this may not only come as a shock to the intellect, in the way the other examples did, but it may also enter much more deeply into the emotional life and irritate the soul. We know that certain things which are of the spirit must always be grasped at this level. We need to consider the following, however: We have to understand that some kind of shadow lies over the connection between the physical illness and the health which gives us strength in the world of the spirit. The connection is a true one, but somehow we feel in our hearts that we cannot really accept this. This has to be admitted. Yet if we really understand the connection it also has another effect, which may be described as follows.

Suppose someone makes a serious effort to absorb the science of the spirit and study it and does so not just in theory, by merely taking in thoughts and ideas, in the way other sciences are studied.

The science of the spirit should become something like a spiritual life blood in us, awakening inner responses and feelings with all the concepts it gives us. For those who have the right ear for this science of the spirit, there is nothing in it which does not either uplift us or allow us to look into the abysses of existence, in order that we may find our bearings in them, too. We may say that those who truly understand the science of the spirit will also always follow everything it has to say with their feelings. If we absorb this science, acquiring the habit of thought and forming ideas, as I have indicated, we actually transform our souls whilst still in the physical world. I have said on a number of occasions that serious study of anthroposophy is one of the best and most effective exercises.

A strange thing happens when people gradually enter more and more into the science of the spirit. If they are doing the exercises, or perhaps do not even do the exercises which will make them into spiritual investigators but make serious efforts to gain real understanding of the science, it may be a very long time before they have any prospect of having clairvoyant vision. They will have it one day, but it may well be a far-off ideal. Yet if you let the science of the spirit influence your soul in the sense I have indicated, you will find that the instincts of life, the more unconscious mainsprings of life, change in the soul. You do not become active in the science of the spirit without it having an influence on the life of instincts, so that it will have different sympathies and antipathies, be filled with light, and feel more secure than it did before.

This may be noticed in every sphere of life. If you are clumsy with your hands, for instance, and become an anthroposophist, you will find that without having done anything but receive the science of the spirit, you become more skilful, even in the way you use your hands. Do not say: 'I know some anthroposophists who are very clumsy; they are far from skilful.' Consider instead how far these individuals have not yet truly made the science of the spirit part of their inner lives, to the extent their karma requires. You may be a painter and have mastered the art of painting up to a point. When you become an anthroposophist, you will find that the influences of which I am speaking flow into the way you instinctively master the art. You find it easier to mix your colours, and the ideas you want come more readily. Or let us assume you are an academic person and supposed to do some scientific work. Many who are in this situation will know how much effort it often takes to collect the literature needed to solve some particular problem. When you become an anthroposophist you will no longer go to libraries and first of all borrow fifty volumes that are of no use, which is what you did before; instead, you will immediately lay your hands on the book you want. Spiritual science has a direct influence on your life; it changes your instincts and gives new mainsprings to life that make you more skilful in life.

What I am now going to say must, of course, always be seen in connection with human karma, for human beings are always subject to karma. However, even if we take this into account, the following is nevertheless true: Let us suppose someone who has entered into the science of the spirit in the way I have described contracts a particular disease and it lies in his karma that he can be cured. It may, of course, be his karma that the disease is incurable. Yet if we are faced with an illness, karma never says in a fatalistic way that it has to take a particular course. The disease can be cured or it cannot be cured. Someone who has steeped himself in anthroposophy acquires an inner instinct which helps him to meet the disease and its accompanying weaknesses with something that will strengthen him and be right for the situation. What will otherwise be experienced as the consequences of the disease in the world of the spirit, will work back into the soul as an instinct whilst you are still in the physical body. You will either prevent the disease or inwardly find your way to the powers that heal.

Clairvoyant consciousness finds the right healing factors for an illness in the following way: The clairvoyant individual is able to have an image of the disease before him. Suppose, then, he has the image before him: here is the disease; it weakens the human being in this particular way. Having clairvoyant consciousness, the individual concerned perceives the counter-image: the mood of overcoming illness and the growing strength welling up from that mood. He sees the compensation which will come to the individual who had the illness in the physical world when he is in the world of the spirit. The clairvoyant is able to give advice based on this. You do not even have to be fully clairvoyant, for the advice to be given may come instinctively from observing the signs of the disease. The process which brings to clairvoyant consciousness the compensation which will indeed come in the world of the spirit belongs to the signs and symptoms of the disease just as much as the upward swing of the pendulum on one side belongs to its upward swing on the other side.

This example clearly shows the connection between the physical plane and the world of the spirit, and shows how fruitful knowledge of that world can be for the conduct of life on the physical plane.

Let us go back to the first concrete example I have given today, which showed that just as the physical world is around us on the physical plane, so the spirit, full of wisdom, is around us in the world of the spirit, an ever-present spiritual element . Now, if we take this from a particular aspect it can throw a very important light on what happens in the world of the spirit. In the physical world we may come across things where we ask ourselves: What is the essential nature of this? How does it act and react? What laws govern this object or process? Or we may walk past them as dullards, asking no questions at all. We shall never learn anything of value unless we let objects arouse questions in us and set riddles for us. Merely looking at them will never take us to the point where the soul becomes its own guide. This is different on the spiritual plane. On the physical plane we put our questions to objects and processes and have to make the effort to investigate them and formulate the answer out of the things themselves. On the spiritual plane, things and realities are around us in the spirit; it is they who put questions to us, not we who put questions to them. They are there; we confront them and are continually questioned by them. It should be possible for us to draw on the infinite ocean of wisdom for everything we need to answer the questions which are put to us. We have to extract the answers not out of the things themselves but out of ourselves, for they put the questions to us; all around us are things that put questions.

Something else has to be taken into account: Let us suppose we are confronting some process or reality in the world of the spirit; this always puts a question to us. We find, however, that we cannot develop the will – will combined with feeling, or feeling combined with will – to enable us to answer the question out of the infinite wisdom, though we know the answers to be in us. Our inner being is infinitely deep; all the answers are there inside us, but we are unable to give the answer. The consequence will be that we rush past in the stream of time and miss the right moment for giving the answer. We have not gained the ability and maturity, perhaps because of our previous development, to answer the question at this point in time. We have been slow to develop in this respect, and would only be able to answer later on. The opportunity will not come again, however; we have missed it. We have failed to use all our opportunities and so we pass by things and events without giving answers to them. We have such experiences all the time in the world of the spirit.

Thus it happens that in the life between death and rebirth we face an entity which puts a question to us. Our lives on earth and the lives in the spirit which came between them have not taken us to the point where we can answer the question when it is put to us. We have to go past and enter into another incarnation. The consequence is that in our next incarnation we have to depend on the good gods to give us, without our being conscious of it, the impulses we need so that we shall not pass by when the same question is put again. This is the way in which things are connected.

I have said on a number of occasions that the further we go back in human evolution the more we are aware that people did not have the mentality we have today but a kind of clairvoyance on the physical plane. Our present way of seeing things has evolved out of a dull, dream-like clairvoyance. If we find people who are still at the primitive, elementary stages of inner development, we find their thinking and feeling still to be more akin to the original clairvoyance. Genuine clairvoyance – I mean primitive, atavistic clairvoyance – is becoming rarer all the time, but in some forms of rural life we still find people who have preserved something from earlier times, so that echoes of the days of earlier clairvoyance still persist. In a dull, dreamlike form, this clairvoyance, in which people see into the worlds of the spirit, has particular features which we also know with developed clairvoyance; this, however, does not show things in a dull, dreamlike way, but clearly and distinctly.

Spiritual science shows us that human beings, as they are in the present cycle of time, must more and more be able to give answers at the right time when questions are put to them in the life between death and rebirth. Their ability to develop in the right way and come closer to the gods' ideal of the perfect human being will depend on this. As I have said, this was experienced in the form of dreams in earlier times, and a vestige of this remains in the themes of numerous fairy-tales and legends, though this is getting less and less. The legends and fairy-tale themes are more or less the following: Such and such a person meets a spirit who keeps putting questions to him which he must answer. He knows that he must answer by the time the clock strikes a certain hour. This is a very common theme. It was the same in the dreamlike clairvoyance of earlier times and now presents itself again in the way I have described in the world of the spirit. Characteristic features of that world are always a wonderful guide to the understanding of myths, legends, fairy-tales and the like, and help us to place them where they belong. This is a point where we can see how evolution has brought us close to the gates of spiritual science, and this is true even for the intellectual life of today.

It is interesting to note that a book which in many respects is well-intentioned, like the one written by my late friend Ludwig Laistner,[1] is unsatisfactory because it fails to deal with the themes relating to the questions which are put in the light of knowledge gained through spiritual science. The author would have needed to know something of how spiritual-scientific truths come into the subject.

Considering the particular instances I have given, we see that something quite specific is demanded in the world of the spirit. It is not a matter of gathering knowledge, as is done on the physical plane, but in fact of reducing knowledge and of transforming power of insight into power of life. You cannot be an investigator in the other world in the same sense as in this world; that would be very much out of place there, for when you are there you can know everything; it is there all around you. What matters is that we develop the will and the feeling towards knowledge and insight which enable us to produce from the whole treasury of our will activity exactly what is needed at a given time to be able to apply the wisdom; otherwise we are smothered or drowned in wisdom. In this world it is essential to think; in the other world it is essential to develop the will combined with feeling which shapes and forms reality out of wisdom and lets it become a kind of creative power. There we have the spirit just as here we have physical nature, and our task is to guide the spirit to physical nature.

A beautiful saying is to be found in the theosophical literature of the first half of the nineteenth century. It comes from Oetinger,[2] who lived at Murrhardt in Wuerttemberg and who was so far advanced in his spiritual development that he was at times able, in full consciousness, to help spiritual entities, that is to say, souls who were not on the physical plane. His words are remarkable and both beautiful and true: 'Spiritual creative power fulfils itself in nature and in nature's forms.' They bring to expression the things for which I have been drawing on the world of the spirit itself. In that world, creative power seeks to bring everything to realization that seethes and surges in wisdom. Here we draw wisdom from reality; in the world of the spirit we do the opposite. The task is to give effect in living realities to what lies in the wisdom. The goal of the gods is reality cast into shape and form.

So we see that it is a matter of feeling suffused with will – or will suffused with feeling – being transformed into creative power; this we have to use in the spiritual world in the same way as here on earth we must make efforts to use our thinking to investigate the physical world and acquire wisdom.

In view of this possibility in the spiritual world, it is essential that we should develop our feeling and thinking in the right way and prepare ourselves here, on the physical plane, in a way appropriate for the present cycle of time. Everything which happens between death and rebirth in the world of the spirit is the consequence of what happens between birth and death in the physical world. True, conditions are so different in the world of the spirit that we must acquire entirely new ideas and concepts if we are to understand that world; nevertheless the two worlds are connected, just as cause and effect are connected. We shall only understand the connections between the spiritual and the physical if we recognize that they have a cause and effect relationship.

The preparations must be made in the physical world. Let us therefore consider the question: How can we prepare ourselves in the right way on the physical plane in the present cycle of time so that – whether we enter the world of the spirit through initiation or through the gate of death – we shall have enough inner power to extract from the wisdom to be found in the world of the spirit what we need to forge realities out of the flowing, surging wisdom? Where can this power be found? It is always important to answer such questions in a way that is right for the particular age. It was different in the times when the way of thinking was such that the earliest and most original sources of the themes found in fairy-tales and legends became accessible. The question is, where do we find the necessary inner power in the present cycle of time?

To help us find the answer, let me mention the following. We may consider a number of different philosophies and try to discover how philosophers arrive at their idea of God. These would of course have to be philosophers who have sufficient depth to let the world convince them that it is possible to speak of a divine principle at work in the world. A nineteenth-century philosopher to be considered is Lotze.[3] He tried to create a philosophy of religion which would be in harmony with the rest of his philosophy. Others, too, had sufficient depth to have what we may call a philosophy of religion. All these philosophers had one particular characteristic. True, with reflections derived from the physical plane, their thinking took them as far as the divine principle; they reflected, did philosophical research, and found – as in the case of Lotze – that the phenomena and entities of the world were maintained by a divine ground which was active in everything and brought it to some degree of harmony. The characteristic feature of these philosophies is that when we take a closer look at this divine ground, the philosophers' god, we find it to be more or less the god who in Hebrew and especially also in Christian religion is called God the Father. Philosophers are able to get as far as this. They can study the physical world and have sufficient depth not to deny the divine principle altogether in the empty-headed way of materialists, and this will take them as far as God the Father. If we study these philosophers we can show quite clearly that philosophical thinking cannot go beyond this God the Father who is seen as the one and only god. Some philosophers – Hegel,[4] for instance – also speak of the Christ, but it is possible to show that this derived not from philosophy but from positive religion. They knew the Christ from positive religion and were therefore able to include him in the discussion. The difference is that whilst God the Father can be found through philosophy it is quite impossible to find the Christ through philosophical thinking.

This is something I would advise you to ponder and give much thought. Rightly understood it takes us into momentous depths of the enquiring mind and questing soul. It is connected with something which is brought to expression in the Christian religion in a beautiful, symbolic image: the relationship of this other god, the Christ, to God the Father is seen as the relationship of the Son to the Father. This signifies much, even if it is merely a symbol. It is interesting that Lotze, for example, could make nothing of it. He wrote that this symbol cannot be taken literally, of course, for it is not possible for one god to be the son of another.[5] But there is something very telling in this symbol. The relationship between father and son is similar to the relationship between cause and effect, for in a way we may find in the father the cause of the son. The son would not be there if the father were not there. One thing has to be taken into account, however: someone who is potentially able to father a son may equally well not have a son but remain son-less. He would still be the same person. 'A' would be the cause, and 'B', the son, the effect. The effect need not necessarily come about, however; the effect results from the cause as a free act. If we study a cause, therefore, and consider it in connection with its effect, we should not merely enquire into the nature of the cause, for that will achieve nothing; instead, we must ask whether the cause is in fact acting as a cause – this is the essential point. It is characteristic of all philosophy that a line of thought is followed; one thought is developed from another, and if one has a first principle one is immediately looking for what follows from it. This is alright for philosophy as such, but it will never lead us to discover the situation which arises if one considers that the cause need not necessarily act as a cause. The essential nature of a cause may be the same, whether it acts as a cause or not. This is the significant truth presented in the symbol of God the Father and God the Son: the Christ is added to the Father as a free creation which is not an inevitable consequence, but a free act presenting itself side by side with the earlier creation; it was also possible for it not to be, and it was not given to the world because the Father had to give a Son to the world, but as a free act, through grace, out of freedom, out of love, presenting itself freely as it is created. The kind of truth which allows us to find God the Father in the way philosophers do will never lead us to God the Son, to the Christ. To come to the Christ, we have to add the truth of faith to the philosophical truth or, because the age of faith is steadily fading, the truth which is reached through clairvoyant investigation. This must first develop in the human soul as a free act.

Thus it has to be said that proof of the existence of God is found if we consider the way in which events happen in the physical world, but the existence of the Christ can never be proved externally by considering the chain of causes and effects. The Christ has been present, and human souls may fail to perceive him if they do not find the strength in themselves to feel and say: Yes, that is the Christ. It is necessary that we actively muster the strength for the impulse of truth which makes us recognize the Christ in the one who was here on earth as the Christ. The other truths, which belong to the realm of God the Father, may be compulsive; we merely have to make the effort to think and be consistent in our thinking – to be a materialist is to lack logic in your thinking. A philosophy of religion – Lotze's or indeed any other – develops when our thinking compels us to arrive at the divine principle. But we can never be made to recognize the Christ by mere philosophy. It has to be a free act, and there are only two possibilities: either we take faith to its ultimate conclusion, or we begin to investigate the world of the spirit.

We take faith to its ultimate conclusion when we say with the Russian philosopher Soloviev,[6] that with all the philosophical truths human beings gain about the world by allowing themselves to be convinced by logic, they do not relate to a truth that is free. It is a higher truth which does not compel us but is a free act: the highest truth which comes through faith. Soloviev sees the greatest dignity in this: The higher truth, which recognizes the Christ, is the truth which works as a free act and not by compulsion. The knowledge which comes for spiritual investigators and for those who understand the science of the spirit is an active knowledge which progresses from thinking to Imagination, Inspiration and Intuition; it becomes inwardly creative and in its creative activity comes to be at home in the worlds of the spirit. It is very much what we must develop, whether we enter the world of the spirit through initiation or through death.

The wisdom which forces itself on us on earth is to be found in the world of the spirit in an abundance that matches the abundance of natural phenomena here on the physical plane. What matters in the world of the spirit is that we have the impulse and the power to make something of that wisdom and create reality out of it. To be freely creative out of wisdom and active in the spirit – this is the impulse which must live in us. We can have this impulse only if we find the right relationship to Christ. The reality of Christ cannot be proved by the external, brain-bound logic of the intellect. He brings himself to realization in us when we acquire spiritual knowledge. Just as spiritual science joins the other science as a free act, so knowledge of the Christ comes when we approach the world into which we enter through spiritual science or by going through the gate of death.

When, in the present cycle of time, we want to enter into the world of the spirit in a fruitful way, that is to say, if we are prepared to die to the physical world, we need the relationship to the world which can be gained by having the right relationship to the Christ. A god such as the God the Father of Christianity can be found by considering the physical world while we are in a physical body. To understand the Christ truly, not the way he has come down through tradition but purely from insight – this is possible only through the science of the spirit. This takes us into the regions which human beings enter when they die – in a symbolic death when they leave the physical body and know themselves as souls out of the body, or by going through the gate of death. We gain the impulses which we will need when we go through the gate of death by finding the right relationship to the Christ. When in the present cycle of time the moment comes to leave the physical body – either by entering into the development which comes with the science of the spirit, or by actually going through the gate of death – we must be able to face the spiritual entity who has come into the world so that we may find the right relationship to this entity. We can find God the Father in the midst of life. We find the Christ when we find the right way to enter into the spirit, that is, to die.

In Christ we die.
In Christo morimur.

LECTURE SEVEN

Between Death and the Cosmic 'Midnight Hour'

Vienna, 13 April 1914

TODAY IT WILL BE NECESSARY TO RETURN to the subject of life between death and rebirth, but now in the light of the ideas developed in the last four lectures. The subject is so vast that much can only be touched on briefly, and some of the things which may not be immediately evident from the images presented will need to be developed later. Anything our anthroposophical friends find incomplete today will be clarified as more knowledge is gained through the science of the spirit.

Human beings have laid aside the physical body when they go through the gate of death; the body is given over to the elements of the earth. We might also say that it has risen above the forces and the laws which come from the essential human being between birth and death, laws which are different from the purely chemical and physical laws to which it becomes subject after death. From the standpoint of the physical world we hold the view, quite naturally, that the part of the essential human being which belongs to the physical plane has remained behind on, or has been given over to, this plane. However, the standpoint which matters for human beings and for understanding the world of the spirit is that of the individual who has had to go through the gate of death. For him, leaving the physical body is an inner process, one which happens in the soul; for those who are left behind, anything which happens to the physical body after death is an external process. The inmost being, the human soul element of the person who has died, no longer comes to expression in the mortal remains. Nevertheless, when a person dies, the inner experience connected with leaving the body is: You have gone out of your physical body and are leaving it behind.

From the standpoint of the physical plane it is extremely difficult to give a true description of what is taking place in the soul at this time, for this is an inner process which essentially is enormously comprehensive and of tremendous significance. It does not take long, but it has universal significance for the whole of human life. It is not yet possible to describe the perceptions gained in the soul at that point in a public lecture, for the general public would be quite shocked; perhaps the time will come when this is possible. The perceptions gained as a new life begins between death and rebirth are, in spiritual terms, outer perceptions; they may be described as follows. At first, individuals who have gone through the gate of death feel: Your relationship to the world is now completely different to what it was before, and fundamentally the whole of your earlier relationship to the world has been completely reversed. To describe the experience they go through we would really have to say: Until they died, human beings lived on the earth; they were used to standing on a solid, physical earth and seeing on this earth the things and creatures belonging to the mineral, plant and animal worlds – mountains, rivers, clouds, stars, sun and moon. From their particular point of view and through the faculties given by their physical bodies they have become accustomed to seeing the whole of this the way people do nowadays, in spite of the fact that Copernicanism has shown it to be essentially an illusion: the blue vault of heaven above us like a shell, covered with stars, with sun and moon passing across it, and so on. We ourselves are inside this shell or hollow sphere; we are at its centre, on the earth, together with everything we are able to perceive on the earth.

What matters now is not that this is an illusion, with the blue sphere around us the product of our limited faculties, but that we cannot help ourselves. The limitations of our faculties make us see a blue sphere as the firmament above us. When human beings have gone through the gate of death, the first thing they must inwardly perceive is this: You are now outside the blue sphere. You are looking at it from the outside and it is as if it has shrunk to a star. Initially there is no awareness of the world of stars into which human beings are actually expanding, but only of the sphere of consciousness which they had when they were in a physical body and everything the human faculties developed in that body allowed them to perceive. It is really – though at a spiritual level – rather like the conscious experience of a chick which is first of all inside the egg and then breaks the shell and sees the broken shell which has been its whole world until now from the outside. The image which passes through the soul at this point is, of course, also maya, but it is a necessary maya. As I said, anything which previously made up the content of our conscious mind has shrunk as if into a star, but now, starting from that star, something spreads out which we may call 'radiant cosmic wisdom'.

I spoke of this radiant cosmic wisdom in the last lecture, saying that we have it in abundance. It shines and glitters towards us as if from a fiery star, not blue now, like the firmament, but fiery, with a reddish glow. The fullness of wisdom radiates from it into space and first of all – being highly mobile in itself – shows us the panorama of the memories of our last life. Everything we have consciously and inwardly experienced between birth and death presents itself to the soul but in such a way that we know: You see it all because the star which grows in radiance before you is the background; its inner activity makes it possible for you to see everything spread out before you in a panorama.

This is the way we would express it from the standpoint of Imagination. From the standpoint of the inner life, the experience is more or less such that the individual who has gone through the gate of death is now entirely filled with the thought: You have left your body. Now, in the world of the spirit, this body is all will. It is a star made of will substance. This will is radiant with heat and reflects to you, who have poured out into the cosmic expanse, your own life between birth and death, so that it is like a vast panorama. Thanks to the fact that you dwelt inside this star, you are able to draw and absorb everything you could from the world when you were on the physical plane. This star of will which now forms the background is the spiritual part of your physical body, it is the spirit which enters into every part of your physical body and fills it with its powers. The wisdom which radiates towards you is the activity, the mobility, of your ether body.

The time when we have the impression that life is presenting itself as a panorama of memories takes only days – I spoke of this also in the public lecture. It is as if the thoughts which became our memories during life on earth unfold and present themselves once more to the inner eye in a panoramic view. We are able to keep it before us for as long as we normally have the power to keep awake in the physical body. It is not a question of the length of time for which we stayed awake under abnormal conditions at some time in life, but of the powers we have within us to keep awake. Some people can hardly keep awake for a single night, whilst others can hold out longer without getting sleepy. This particular power determines the length of time individuals need to go through the whole panorama. We also have the distinct inner consciousness that because the star of will is in the background, the panorama contains the achievements of our last life on earth. It contains what we accomplished in the way of becoming more mature and have taken through death, as it were, as an addition to the endowment with which our life began. And we have the feeling that this, which we may call the fruit of our last life, will not remain as it was during the panoramic review; we feel as though it were moving away and disappearing into the distant ages of future time.

Today I shall speak mainly of the life between death and rebirth of human beings who have lived the normal length of life and died under normal circumstances. Details relating to exceptional cases will be given tomorrow.

Any fruit we have gained in life thus draws away into the distance and we know in our souls that it somehow exists but that we have remained behind. We are aware of remaining at an earlier point in time; the fruit of life moves away quickly, so that it will reach a later point in time before us and we have to follow in its wake. This inner experience of the fruit of life dwelling in the universe must be brought to mind strongly, for it is the basis of our consciousness after death. Conscious awareness always has to be aroused by something. When we wake up in the morning, having been unconscious during sleep, conscious awareness is fanned into life by the process of entering into the physical body and now facing things that are outside us and have an influence from outside. In the situation which exists immediately after death, consciousness is fanned into life by feeling and living our way into the fruit which has been gained in the last life. This exists, but it is outside now. Feeling and living our way into our inmost being, as it was on earth, our consciousness comes alive after death.

Then comes a time when it is necessary to develop inner powers which essentially have had to remain undeveloped during life on earth, because they were then used to organize the physical body and therefore also our whole life on earth. After death these powers in the soul must gradually wake up, and some of this actually happens during the days when we are experiencing the panorama of memories. The panorama gradually fades away, and this is because we then develop the powers which underlie the ability to remember but do not come to conscious awareness in physical life, because they have to be transformed in that life to enable us to create memories. The last great memory, which takes the form of the panorama after death, must die down and fade away, and then something we were not able to hold in conscious awareness develops out of the twilight. Before death, these powers were transformed into the power of memory; now the possibility of remembering earthbound thoughts in the usual way has been overcome and they emerge. The power of memory, now transformed into a spiritual power, emerges from the human soul after death just as powers of the soul emerge in a growing child. As it develops after death, we perceive that behind the thoughts, which on the physical plane were mere shadow images, lies something which is alive and that the world of thought is full of life and activity. We become aware that in truth a host of elemental spirits is spreading out behind it. Thus we see our memories fade away and a host of elemental spirits awakening out of the cosmos of universal wisdom to take their place.

You may ask: Surely it will be a loss for us when the power of memory is overcome and we have something else instead? We do not lose anything, for there is plenty to replace it. Instead of recalling our thoughts, as we do in life, we find that those thoughts merely appeared to be memories. Our treasured store of memories now turns out to be something entirely different. When we are out of the physical body we see the whole of this store of memories as a living, immediate reality. Every thought is a living elemental spirit. Now we know: During life on earth, you thought it was your own thoughts which came to mind. But while you were under the illusion of creating your own thoughts you were actually creating elemental spirits. This is the new contribution you have made to the cosmos. Something which has been born out of you and into the spirit now shows itself and you know what your thoughts were in reality. At this point you gain direct perception of the nature of elemental spirits, and you do so by first of all recognizing the elemental spirits you yourself have created.

The memory panorama is the first significant experience after death. It comes to life, however, actually comes to life, and in doing so it is transformed into a host of elemental spirits. It may now be said to show its true face, and disappears by changing into something entirely different. If, for example, we have died at the age of sixty or eighty, we no longer need the power of memory for a thought we may have had at the age of twenty. That thought is now a living elemental spirit; it has been waiting there and we do not need to recall it. If we had died at the age of forty, for instance, the thought would be only twenty years old, and this is clearly apparent. These elemental spirits tell us of their own accord how long ago they were created. Time now becomes space. We have it before us when the living spirits show us their own time signatures. Time becomes the immediate present in these circumstances.

Our own elemental spirits were around us in life and we see them in death. They reveal to us the true nature of the elemental world in general and also prepare us to understand elemental spirits from the outside world as they gradually enter our field of vision. Those spirits were not created by us; they exist without us in the spiritual cosmos. Elemental spirits of our own creation help us to know others.

Just try to imagine how utterly different life between death and rebirth is from the life we know on earth. Immediately after birth the human being has no self awareness. The experiences of an infant are those of the people around him. He has been born, and others, his parents, look at the being who has been born. After death we do not look at ourselves to begin with, but we see something to which we have given birth at the moment of death. When we enter into the physical world, the outside world is incomprehensible to us and our own movements and cries – and chuckles, too – are really only there for others. After death, which means being born into the world of the spirit, we are first of all in an environment to which we ourselves have given birth; we build this up around us because we have given birth to it. There we have given birth to our world; when we are born into physical life the world gives birth to us. This, then is what happens to our thoughts and what becomes of them when they are our store of memories.

It is different with feeling and will. In the lecture I gave on 9 April I said that anything belonging to the sphere of feeling and will has not yet come to birth in its full reality. This becomes particularly evident after death because the will and feeling which were in the physical body are still in existence. After a time, therefore, when the star of will and the fruits of the last life on earth have moved away, the human soul lives in an elemental environment which takes its fundamental note from the transformed memories. Living in this world — which in the sense of which we have spoken is he himself — the human being knows: Your feeling and will are still alive in you; they now have a kind of memory, a kind of link, with the last life on earth. This continues for decades. On earth, between birth and death, we have pleasure and pain and live in our passions and develop will impulses because we have a soul which feels and has a will. Yet the full potential of feeling and will can never develop in the body. We may live to a ripe old age but the truth is that when we die we could still have had more pleasure, more pain and could have developed more will impulses. The potential of feeling and will which remains in the soul must first be overcome. Until this is done, we are tied to our last life by powerful desires.

We look back on our last life on earth. I have often said that in commonplace terms it is as if we have to be weaned from our connection with physical life. Anyone who is even a little bit a scientist of the spirit will soon perceive the true nature of the power which has to be overcome at this stage — which usually continues for decades — for it is relatively accessible to that science.

Every night when we go to sleep after the experiences of the day, our soul and spirit are outside the body for the period between going to sleep and waking up. We return because our soul and spirit have the instinct to return. We literally hanker after the body, and if you are able to have conscious experience of the waking-up process you know: You want to wake up and indeed must want to wake up. The spirit and the soul thus are subject to the force of attraction which draws them to the body. After death this must gradually fade away and be overcome. It takes decades to do so, and it is the reason why our after-death experiences have to come indirectly during this time, through our previous life on earth.

Having given the preceding lectures, I am now in a position to describe some things in more detail, rather than give the general overview which is all that is usually possible; a more detailed description is only possible when the necessary concepts have been developed.

Suppose we ourselves have gone through the gate of death and left someone behind on earth. We are now living in the period where we are able to see into the elemental spirits and develop a feeling for our own reality, knowing that the fruits of our life on earth have drawn away into the distance. The connection with that life on earth continues, however. Let us suppose we have left behind someone very dear to us. Our own elemental creations help us to become accustomed to perceiving the elemental spirits which others have created by having thoughts. Thanks to our own elemental spirits we gradually learn to see what those we have left behind are thinking; we see the thoughts which live in them, for these present themselves to the inner eye in mighty Imaginations. We are therefore able to connect much more with the inner life of the person concerned than was possible in the physical world. We were not able to perceive the thoughts of others when we were in physical bodies; now we are able to do so. But we need to recall the feelings we had in our last life on earth and relate to them. We have to be able to feel what we felt when we were in a body; this feeling must linger on, and this will give life to a relationship which otherwise would merely be like relating to a picture representing the thoughts of the other person. A living connection is thus made through our feelings, and fundamentally speaking, it is the same with everything else.

You see, it is a process of working ourselves out of a condition in which we still have to draw on our last life on earth for the powers we need to enter into living relationship with our spiritual environment; the connection with that life on earth must still be there. We love those we have left behind, and the thoughts which live in them appear to us as elemental spirits; we love them because we ourselves are still depending on the love we had for them during life on earth. There is something which goes against the grain in using expressions such as the following, but some of you will understand what I mean by saying: Life on earth – not the life of thought, but the inner feelings imbued with will impulses with which we are still connected – becomes like an electrical relay system through which our own inner being can perceive and relate to the life of the spirit which surges around us. We really feel ourselves living further on into time, rather like a time comet. Our previous earth life has become like a kernel which develops something like a comet's tail extending into the near future and we live in that tail. We are still connected with our life on earth in so far as it is filled with feeling and will. Out of this experience, something must be born in the inner life which is not immediate feeling and will. The powers of feeling and of will which we develop in the physical world owe their form to the fact that we are in a physical body. When the soul is no longer in a physical body it must develop other faculties which lie dormant during physical life. With the effect of feeling and will lingering on for years, the soul must bring the powers of desire with feeling, or feeling with desire, to maturity which it can use in this connection in the world of the spirit. We know that our feeling and our will are alive in the soul; but essentially they do not help us after death, they must gradually fade and die away. They do so after a period of some years. But something must develop in the process which can be of service after death.

Our thoughts then live outside us as elemental spirits. The feeling and will which formerly lived in us would be of no use to us in this world which we ourselves are and which is outside us. We must – and indeed do – gradually develop a will which pours and streams out of us and seethes and surges towards the place where our living thoughts are. It enters into them because feeling, which is entirely inside us during physical life, is borne on the waves of the will. Out there seethes and surges the ocean of our will, and on it floats feeling. When the will encounters an elemental thought-spirit, the collision which occurs sets feeling aglow and we become aware of this rebound of our will as an absolute reality in the world of the spirit.

What I mean is this: Let us suppose there is an elemental spirit in the spiritual environment. When we have worked our way out of the condition which must first be gone through, the will which is then coming from us surges towards this elemental spirit and is thrown back when it comes up against it. It returns to us not as will but as feeling, streaming back to us in the ocean of will. Our true self, poured out into the cosmos, lives as feeling which returns to us on the waters of the will. This is how the elemental spirits become real to us and we gradually become more and more aware of our spiritual environment.

But another power must also develop; this lies dormant in far deeper layers of the soul than feeling combined with will, or will combined with feeling. It is the creative power of the soul which is like a light which must shine out into the world of the spirit. With this, we shall not merely see the objective thought spirits which are alive and active as they return on the waves of the will ocean, but also have the world of the spirit illumined with the light of the spirit. A creative, spiritual power of light gradually awakens in us and goes out into the world of the spirit.

You see, when we are in a physical body, feeling and will, which are like brother and sister, are two distinct entities; when we have gone through the gate of death they are one. The creative power we radiate into space in the world of the spirit – if I may call it 'space', for it is not really space; I have to use the term as an analogy to help you to understand how things are in that world – this light of the soul lies dormant deep down in us, for it is connected with something we cannot and must not know about during life. It is then redeemed to become the light which illumines the world of the spirit. In physical life this principle must be transformed and used in such a way that our body is truly alive and the bearer of consciousness. Deep down below the level of consciousness this power of light is active in the physical body, organizing both life and consciousness. We must not allow it to enter into earthly consciousness, for this would rob the body of the power which organizes it. Now, when we do not have a body which needs to be taken care of, it becomes light of the spirit, radiating, illuminating everything and filling it with glittering light. These words signify absolute realities.

Thus we gradually come to be at home in the world of the spirit and experience it as a real world, just as the physical world is real to us here and now. Our work gradually takes us to the point where we truly have as our companions the souls of those who have died, in so far as they are living in the world of the spirit. We live among them, just as here in the physical body we live among other bodies. When we penetrate more and more to the true inner essence of spiritual science it sounds foolish to us when someone asserts that we shall not meet again all the people whom we knew in life. It sounds as foolish as if someone were to say that we do not find any people when we come to earth at birth. People are here all around us. For someone who has knowledge of life in the spirit, it is as if someone were to say: The child grows into the world but it does not see people. This is obviously nonsense. It is equally nonsensical for people to say: When we enter into the world of the spirit we do not find again all the souls with whom we were connected, nor do we find the entities of the higher hierarchies. We gradually come to know them just as we come to know minerals, plants and animals here on earth. The difference is that here we know that when we see or hear things, the possibility of doing so, of using our senses, comes from the outside world. In the world of the spirit we know that the possibility lies in us; the element we may call the radiant light of the soul streams out from us and shines both on and through everything around us.

Thus we live on into the time which may be called the first half of life between death and a new birth, going through the two stages of which I have also spoken in the public lecture. One of these takes years. Letting the light of the soul shine out we relate to the world of the spirit by perceiving the spirits and the souls around us. This gradually fades and we feel: You are now less and less able to develop the power of light in the soul and must allow it to grow dim and progressively darker, in a spiritual sense. The result is that you see less of the spiritual entities. As time goes on this stage alternates with times when you say to yourself: The spiritual entities are all around you, but you are becoming increasingly more solitary; all you have is the content of your inner life, and this grows all the richer the more you grow unable to illumine the entities around you. There are periods of spiritual sociability and periods when we live over again in the soul what we experienced during the sociable period. They alternate, like the swing of the pendulum.

During times of spiritual solitude we know: Everything you experienced all around you was indeed there; you know about it. Now, however, you have only echoes of it. We might say that during the periods of solitude we have memories, but this does not entirely meet the case. Let me try, therefore, and present it to you from another point of view.

The experience we have is not as if we were remembering what we experienced in the world of the spirit, but as if we had to produce it all over again at every moment: it is a process of continuous activity. But you know that whilst the outside world is out there, you need to be alone with yourself and in continuous activity. What you produce is the world surging around you beyond the shores of your own being.

As we live on during the first half of life between death and a new birth and approach the middle of this period, we feel the life of inner solitude grow richer and richer, with the periods when we look out into the spiritual environment getting shorter, as it were, and dimmer, until we reach the midpoint of life between death and rebirth. I have tried to represent this 'cosmic midnight hour' in my last Mystery Play *The Soul's Awakening*. This is the time when the inner life reaches its greatest intensity, but we no longer have the creative power to illumine our spiritual environment. Infinite worlds arising out of our own being may fill our spirit, but we know of no reality of being other than our own. This is the cosmic midnight hour which comes at the midpoint of life between death and a new birth.

Now comes the time when the longing for a positive creative power arises. We have an infinitude as our inner life, but the longing comes to have an outside world once more. Conditions differ so much between the world of the spirit and the physical world that longing, which is the most passive of all powers in the physical world, where the object of our longing rules our life, is the opposite in the other world. There it becomes a creative power; it changes into a new kind of inner light that will give us an outside world which, however, is also an inner world, for our eyes are opened to our earlier incarnations on earth. These now spread before us, illumined by the light born of our longing. There is a power in the spiritual cosmos which can illumine those past lives for us out of our longing and let us experience them. One thing is needed for this, however, in our present cycle of time.

I have told you that during the whole of the first half of life between death and rebirth we alternate between inner life and outer life, solitude and spiritual sociability. To begin with, conditions in the world of the spirit are such that each time we return to the state of solitude, our inner activity is to recall what we have experienced in the outside world. This brings about a state of consciousness which spreads over the whole world of the spirit as though on wings of infinity. The wings are closed up again in the period of solitude.

One thing must remain, however, irrespective of whether we spread out over the great world of the spirit or withdraw from it. Before the Mystery of Golgotha, the powers which connected human beings with primordial times enabled them to have firm coherence of ego and not lose it; this means that it was possible to remember clearly at all times that in this life on earth you were an 'I'. This memory must continue through the periods of solitude and sociability. Before the Mystery of Golgotha provision was made for this through powers of heredity. Now, however, provision can only be made if a connection is maintained between the fruits of our earth life, which we felt move away from us as soon as we left the physical body, and the inner fulfilment which can be ours because Christ has poured himself into the earth's aura. If we fill ourselves with Christ substance this will enable us to remember our ego through the transition from life to death and until we come to the cosmic midnight hour; we shall remember it, however much we expand into the world of the spirit and contract into solitude. The impulse coming from the Christ power which helps us not to lose ourselves reaches that far. Then, however, a new power of spirit must fan our longing so that new light arises. This power exists only in the life of the spirit.

In the physical world we have the world of nature and the divine principle present in this, out of which we are born into the physical world. The Christ impulse is present in the aura of physical nature on earth. But the power which comes to us at the cosmic midnight hour and makes our longing shine out and illumine the whole of our past – this power exists only in the world of the spirit, where physical bodies cannot live. The Christ impulse has taken us as far as the cosmic midnight hour, and this midnight hour has been experienced by the soul in solitude of spirit. Cosmic darkness has developed because the light of the soul can no longer shine out from us. Now a spiritual power arises out of the cosmic midnight hour and out of our longing; it creates a new cosmic light, making our own true nature luminous, and we are able to take hold of ourselves and awaken again in cosmic existence. We come to know the spirit of the spiritual world which now awakens us as a new light shines out from the cosmic midnight hour and illumines our human past. We have died in Christ. Through the spirit, a spirit which has no body – the technical term for this is 'the Holy Spirit', 'holy' meaning to live without a body – and does not have the weaknesses of a spirit which lives in a body, our own true nature is reawakened out of the cosmic midnight hour.

Thus we are awakened by the Holy Spirit at the cosmic midnight hour.

Per spiritum sanctum reviviscimus.

LECTURE EIGHT

Pleasures and Sufferings in the Life Beyond

Vienna, 14 April 1914

IN THIS LAST LECTURE I SHOULD LIKE to continue from where we left off yesterday. We were speaking of the great cosmic midnight hour of spiritual existence between death and a new birth, when inner experience reaches its greatest intensity, and spiritual sociability – which is our connection with the outside world in the spirit – is at its lowest ebb, so that in a certain respect spiritual darkness surrounds us. It was also said that the longing for the outside world becomes active again and that this happens through the spirit which is active in the world of the spirit. This longing causes a new light of soul to stream out from us, enabling us to see an outside world of quite specific character.

The outside world we see then is our own past, that is, our previous incarnations and periods when we were between death and a new birth. We look back on everything we gained through world existence, and everything we still owe to it. Two things come before us with particular vividness. We have enjoyed many of the pleasures and delights of existence – this is revealed as it were in spiritual vision, but in a way that reveals the spiritual value; we see what these things have made of us.

Let us take a concrete example. We look back on something we enjoyed and which has given us satisfaction in one of our past lives, and feel that although it lies behind us in time it is not a thing of the past. Its effect continues into all future ages in such a way that it awaits what we are going to make of it.

Looking back like this, the immediate experience in the soul is that the pleasure we enjoyed must become a power in the soul which may be given effect in two ways. In your life in the spirit after the cosmic midnight hour you have two possibilities, and the spiritual world simply provides you with the abilities to bring one of them to realization. You can transform your past pleasure and satisfaction into the ability to develop the inner power which enables you to achieve something that will be of value to the world; it may be something very small or something great. This is the one possibility. The other is that we may say to ourselves: I have had the pleasure and I am going to be content with this; I shall take it into my soul and bask in the fact that I have had this experience. If we choose this possibility with many things which have given us pleasure and satisfaction we create a power in us that will gradually cause our spirit to be stifled and to degenerate. One of the most important things we can learn in the world of the spirit is that our pleasure and satisfaction also put us in debt with world existence. The prospect arises before the eye of the spirit that if we do not make the decision at the right time to create abilities to do something of value in life our spirit will be stifled. Here you are again able to see that the spiritual element and anything which happens on the physical plane interact with each other.

If we make the science of the spirit increasingly our own, in the sense we discussed in the lecture on 12 April, it will become part of our instinctive life. Something like the stirring of conscience will then induce the following mood when we experience pleasures and satisfactions on the physical plane: It is wrong to accept a pleasure or delight merely for your own pleasure. Instead we shall let a feeling of gratitude to the universe and the powers of spirit in the universe enter into our pleasure. We shall know that every pleasure and delight puts us in debt to the universe. We shall find it easiest to transform pleasures of the mind and spirit. Pleasures which need the body as an instrument for their achievement, or will altogether only come because we have a body here on the physical plane, will also present themselves as something which needs to be transformed during the period indicated between death and rebirth, to prevent ourselves becoming stifled by them. We feel the need to transform them but we also feel that it will take many incarnations, and we can work at this whenever we are in the world of the spirit between those incarnations until we finally achieve the transformation.

We also find something else in the world of the spirit. In the present cycle of human evolution some of our pleasures cause the soul and spirit to be wholly caught up in them on the physical plane; these pleasures have subhuman, if not animal, character – it is possible for pleasure and enjoyment to become subhuman. These cause infinite pain to certain entities in the world of the spirit, entities we shall only meet when we enter into that world. When we are in that world and perceive the pain we cause them we shall be utterly dismayed and depressed, and the powers this creates in the soul will make it very difficult for us to bring harmony into our work, of establishing the conditions for our next incarnation.

With regard to the pain and suffering we have borne on earth – to look on the other side – we find these continue to act on the spiritual plane and fill the soul with powers which become powers of will. This gives strength to the soul, and we have the opportunity to transform this into a moral strength which we can take with us again to the physical plane. The result is that we then have not only the ability to create something of value for the world, but also the moral strength to bring this ability to full expression and give it character.

Those and many others are the experiences we have immediately after the midnight hour of existence in the spirit. We realize the value we have gained in the past and we develop a feeling for the abilities we may have in the future. We then live on in the world of the spirit, and after a time a clear vision emerges from

Lecture Eight 141

the twilight of the spiritual environment. This concerns not only our own past lives but everything human which was closely connected with them. Human souls with whom we had a connection during earlier stages of existence enter into a spiritual relationship with us. This does not mean we did not previously experience the bond – during by far the greater part of the time between death and rebirth we are always aware of those who were close to us in life – but now, as we meet them again after the midnight hour of existence in the spirit, it becomes very clear what we owe to them and what they owe to us. Now we do not merely realize: you had such a relationship to such and such a person during such and such a time – this is something we realized before – but they become the expression for us of compensation for those earlier experiences. We look at them and see the new experiences on the physical plane which will compensate the debt we owe to others, or whatever it may be. We are able to see the future effects of our dealings with them in the past. It will be much easier to understand this if we take a concrete example.

Let us again assume that we have lied to someone. Now is the time in the world of the spirit when the possibility arises of our being tormented by the truth which is the opposite of that lie. What happens is that our relationship to the individual concerned changes so much each time we see him – and we shall see him often enough with the eye of the spirit – for him to make the truth which is the opposite of the lie to arise in us as a torment. The inclination then arises deep down in us to meet the person again on earth and do something to compensate for the wrong we have done by telling the lie. It is not possible to make up for our wrongs in the world of the spirit; we merely gain clear understanding of the effect which a lie has had. Anything of this kind done on earth must be made up for again on earth. We also know that to balance things out we need powers which we can only gain by entering into an earthly body again. Thus the inclination comes to incarnate in a body on earth which will make it possible to balance out our earlier imperfections. If we do not, the person concerned will appear again when we have gone through our next death and cause the torment of the truth to return. Here you have the whole spiritual technique of creating the urge in us to compensate karma.

Compensation is also made for other reasons; but I would have to present thousands of cases to show everything connected with this important question of karma. Consider the following case, for example. Let us suppose the way we are in the world of the spirit after the midnight hour of existence is such that we look back to certain pleasures we have had and say: We can transform the effects of these into abilities which we shall be able to put into effect when we are in our next incarnation. But then the following may happen: We may find that certain elemental spirits are obstructing us as we are transforming past experiences into abilities. This may be the case. The elementals may prevent us from really developing those abilities. We may ask ourselves what can be done: If I give way to these elementals which are approaching and which cannot endure it that these abilities develop in me, I shall not be able to develop them. But this is something I must do. I know that I shall only be able to perform particular services for certain people in my next incarnation if I have these abilities. The general rule is that one develops the abilities in such a case, but this hurts the elementals who are all around us and in a certain way they feel we are attacking them. In particular they feel their own existence darkened when this happens, as if some of their own wisdom were taken from them. One of the consequences will often be that when we are reborn we shall find one or more individuals on earth to be possessed by those elementals and inspired with particularly hostile intentions towards us.

Think how deeply this enables us to look into human 5experience, and the thorough understanding of human life it gives us, teaching us to acquire the right instinct which will make us take the right attitude on the physical plane. It does not mean, however, that we say to ourselves on the physical plane: I had to protect myself at that time; this has made me these enemies and I must now let them have their way. There may be situations where it is good to let them have their way, but there are others where the hostile elementals, allowed to achieve their aims by working through particular people, gain more than compensation for the deprivation suffered when we had to protect ourselves. They overstep the mark, and as a result we would not be able to save ourselves from them when it comes to that time in the period between death and rebirth; in a certain way they would then give the death-blow to certain abilities we might develop.

The world becomes more and more complicated when we gain real insight into it. This should not really surprise us. Let me give you a few more isolated examples of the karmic connections between life on earth and life between death and a new birth. One situation would be that a disease, say, causes death to come early. The individual then retains certain powers which he would have brought to realization if he had lived out the full life span. These residual powers, which the individual could have used if he had not died early, remain. Spiritual investigation of life after death has shown that these powers are added to the powers of will and feeling and increase them. After the midnight hour of existence the individual concerned will be able to use the powers added before the midnight hour and enter life on earth as a more powerful person, with more character and power of will than he would have had if he had not died such an early death. This happens out of karmic necessity, and it would of course be utter foolishness to imagine that we can achieve the same thing by bringing about an early death artificially. You will find the necessary details of what happens when early death is brought on artificially in my book *Theosophy*.[1]

I have also spoken of the case where someone dies young due to an accident.[2] If an accident tears someone away from life on the physical plane where he had sufficient powers to live longer, this again leaves a residue of powers; after the midnight hour of existence this residue is added in such a way that he is able to use it for his powers of intellect. Spiritual investigations have shown that great inventors have often died from an accident in earlier incarnations.

Examples like these show that if we want to gain real understanding of these things we really have to accept that in the world of the spirit the point of view is utterly different from the physical world. You will come to realize more and more that if we are to understand the world of the spirit we must acquire new concepts and ideas, for the worlds of the spirit are utterly different from the physical world. It therefore should not surprise us if something we are told about the world of the spirit at first gives us a feeling of disappointment. One fact which has been frequently confirmed through spiritual investigation is that when a materialist dies and leaves others behind who are also materialists, he will first of all suffer a certain degree of deprivation in the world of the spirit. Having never given thought to the spirit before going through the gate of death, and wanting to look back to his loved ones on earth, whose souls also have no thought of the spirit, he cannot do so directly; his knowledge of them will not go beyond the time when he went through death. The eye of the spirit cannot see what lives in them on earth, for only the life of the spirit casts a light which can be seen in the worlds of the spirit and they have none of this. The individual concerned will have to wait until he has developed the powers in the world of the spirit to enable him to see the matter clearly. He will then see that the souls he has left behind are materialists because they are in the grip of Ahriman. We would be unable to bear it if we experienced this immediately after death. We have to grow into the way in which Ahriman possesses materialistic souls; then we can begin to see them until they, too, have gone through the gate of death and free themselves from their materialistic attitude in the world of the spirit. In this case, one only feels connected with them at a later time.

Someone might say that the conditions I am describing as happening after death are far from comforting, but people only say this because it is an idea acquired on the physical plane and lacks understanding of the worlds of the spirit. Between death and a new birth the dead individual always reaches a point where he says to himself: It would be utterly miserable to see these souls immediately after death if one were a materialist. It clearly is best for all these souls to go through this period of trial first. Otherwise they would lose themselves and be unable to achieve what has to be achieved. The point of view changes completely when we see the things of the world in their spiritual aspect, and a time will come when people will need to have real understanding of the truths of spiritual science whilst still on the physical plane.

The science of the spirit is in the world today because human evolution demands that full understanding of the worlds of the spirit and conditions of existence in them comes alive more and more in human souls, instinctively at first and then in full consciousness.

Let me draw your attention to a purely external phenomenon which will show you that it will happen more and more that people are only able to appreciate the true nature of life on the physical plane if they understand the laws of existence in the spirit. It is very much an external phenomenon, but it is tremendously important.

When we look at the natural world, we note the remarkable fact that only a small number of seeds, or eggs, are ever used to reproduce a life form, and vast numbers of them perish. Of the myriads of spawn in the sea, only a few grow into fishes; the rest perish. We look at a field and see vast multitudes of grains of corn. Only a few of them will grow into plants, the rest perish as seeds when they are used for human food and other purposes. The amount which has to be produced in nature is enormously in excess of anything which enters into the steadily flowing stream of existence to become truly fruitful and germinate again.

This is a wise provision, for order and necessity in nature are such that anything taken out of its own stream of existence and of fruit-bearing is used to serve the other ongoing stream of existence. Creatures would not be able to live if every seed and egg were to become fruitful and develop into a plant or animal. Seed must be there to provide the soil, so to speak, out of which creation may grow. It is maya, illusion, to think something is lost; nothing, in truth, is lost in the workings of nature. The spirit is active in the natural world and the phenomenon of apparent loss from the onflowing stream of evolution is founded in the wisdom of the spirit. It is spiritual law and must be considered from the standpoint of the spirit. If we do so we shall soon discover that the things which are apparently taken out of the onflowing stream have good reason to exist. This provision is founded in the spirit, and insofar as we live the life of the spirit we are able to perceive its true value on the physical plane.

Consider the following, which concerns us closely. Public lectures on the science of the spirit must be given. The audiences for these have simply come in response to publicity. The situation is similar to that of grains of corn, only some of which are used in the ongoing stream of existence. We cannot let ourselves be put off by the fact that the streams of spiritual life have to be presented to large numbers of people, apparently brought together at random, when only a few of them will separate out and actually enter into this life of the spirit, become anthroposophists and join the ongoing stream. The fact is that the seed which is scattered reaches many people who may well walk home after a lecture saying: I think that man was talking a lot of nonsense! Seen in direct relation to external life, this is analogous to the spawn which is lost in the sea. People who have come to a lecture because of their karma and consider the lecturer to have talked nonsense are not yet ready to receive the truth of the spirit, but their souls have need to feel the powers inherent in spiritual science wing towards them in their present incarnation. They may be as abusive as they like; the power will remain with them for their next incarnation, so that the seeds are not lost but find their way. Existence follows the same spiritual laws, irrespective of whether we look for the spiritual element in the order of nature, or in the example I have given, which is of direct concern to ourselves.

But now let us suppose we wanted to apply the same principle in external, material life, and were to say: Well, this is exactly what people are doing in everyday life. Yes, my friends, that is just it; what I am now going to describe is indeed happening and we are moving towards a future where it will happen more and more. People are producing more and more goods; they are building factories without ever asking: How much will be needed? This used to be the case when you had a village tailor who only made a suit when it was ordered. In those days the consumer would say how much had to be produced; today goods are produced for the market, piling up as much as possible. Production functions entirely on the productive principle which applies in the world of nature, and this is now also applied in the social order. For a time this will become more and more widespread. But we are in the realm of matter here. The law of the spirit does not apply in outer life, for it applies only to the world of the spirit. The outcome of this will be something very peculiar. We are speaking among ourselves today and therefore these things can be said. The world will not yet understand this.

Goods are produced for the market regardless of actual consumption. Instead of following the principles discussed in my essay 'Anthroposophy and the Social Question',[3] the tendency is to produce goods by using the money markets, pile them up in warehouses and wait to see how much people will buy. The tendency will increase until it destroys itself – you will see why if you listen to what I am going to say next. With this kind of production becoming part of social life, something will develop in the social context which is like a carcinoma in a human organism. Exactly the same – a carcinoma, a cancer of our civilization! Someone able to see through social life with the eye of the spirit will see the terrible foundations of social cancers, social ulcers springing up everywhere, and the seer feels deep concern for our civilization. Even if one were able to suppress all the enthusiasm one feels for the science of the spirit and anything else requiring one to tell people about it, this terrible thing, which weighs so heavily, is enough to make one want to shout aloud and tell the world the cure for this evil, which is gathering more and more strongly and will grow in power. In the spreading of spiritual truths there is an element which on its own ground must work as nature works, but this way of working becomes a cancer when it enters into civilization in the way I have described.

It will only be possible to see this clearly and find ways of changing it if the science of the spirit takes hold of human hearts and enters into human souls. Being able to see these things, I wish I had words of great power and fire so that I could make everybody else today aware of the time which is approaching. These things can only be understood if we get to know the different points of view, considering now the one field of existence and then the other. When we are experiencing the things which come between the midnight hour and a new birth we have these other points of view, for it is through them that we ourselves must become creative.

When we have developed the inclinations needed to fulfil karma with regard to the experiences which are most immediate, other experiences, which are less immediate, will arise. We experience religious and other communities to which we belonged in such a way that they show us: In your next incarnation you will have to do this or that to prevent yourself from becoming one-sided. In short, life still continues in alternating states of sociability and solitude in spirit, but essentially it serves to create the archetype, or model, for a new life on earth, to begin with as a purely spiritual form.

We have created the spiritual and etheric archetype out of the world of the spirit long before we come down into a life on earth. It contains forces which we may call forces of spiritual magnetism and which draw us to the parents who we feel will give us the hereditary attributes which will allow us to enter into life on earth. I have already indicated that the normal time for this is when we feel we are uniting with the fruit of our last life which had previously moved away from us. However, human beings do not always reach this point. If we were to reach this point our life would be such that we should be fully aware of the relationship between the living physical body and the spiritual element. But most people are premature births with regard to the spirit. However, this will be made up for later by experiences which allow us to be in full harmony again with the fruits of earlier lives on earth.

Yesterday I spoke of something particularly important. At the midnight hour of existence in the spirit, when our longing for the outside world must be greatest, because we have gone most deeply into solitude, the spirit which only seethes and moves and lives in the worlds of the spirit comes and transforms our longing into a kind of light of the soul. Up to this point we must keep the connection with our ego, remembering, as it were: You were this 'I' on earth. We are able to do this in the present cycle of time because the Christ brought into the earth's aura the power that enables us to keep remembering this until the midnight hour. Without the Christ, we could not have taken this power with us from life on earth. A schism, a split, would cause disharmony in our existence halfway between death and a new birth, if the Christ impulse were not flowing through the earth world. We would forget, long before we came to the midnight hour, that we were an 'I' in our last life. We would be aware of the relationship with the world of the spirit, but we would forget our own identity.

The reason for this is that we develop our ego so powerfully on earth. Since the Mystery of Golgotha it has become necessary for us to have growing ego consciousness. But in doing so we use up the powers we shall need after death so that we shall not forget our identity before we come to the midnight hour. To be able to hold on to the memory we must die into Christ. The Christ impulse had to come, for it enables us not to forget our own identity before we reach the midnight hour.

At the midnight hour, the spirit comes to us. If we still remember our identity until the Holy Spirit draws near and gives us the ability to look back and gain a relationship to our own inner world as if it were an outside world, the spirit is able to guide us from then on until we incarnate again, having created our archetype in the world of the spirit.

In reality, of course, we do not normally only limit ourselves to essentials. Just as a pendulum is not at rest but swings to one side and then the other, and it is right that this should happen, so the Christ impulse provides us not only with enough power to enable us to make the connection; under certain circumstances the Christ impulse provides so much power that this could sweep us across if the spirit did not approach us. True, in that case we would not be able to make the connection with our memory, but the Christ impulse would sweep us through. This is of great significance, and in future it will be more and more necessary for humanity to receive an impulse which goes well beyond the limit of what is necessary. Even now it is necessary for people not only to learn the absolute essentials about the Christ but for the Christ impulse to become a powerful impulse in their souls which will sweep them through the midnight hour of existence. This causes the impulse of the spirit to be strengthened with the impulse which comes from the Christ, so that we carry the impulse of the spirit more strongly through the second half of life between death and a new birth than we would if there were no Christ impulse.

The surplus Christ impulse strengthens the impulse of the spirit. Otherwise the spirit would live for the spirit only and cease to be when we are born. If we fill ourselves with the Christ impulse, this enhances the impulse of the Holy Spirit. The result will be that an impulse of the spirit enters into the soul which will be a power which we shall not use up as we use up other powers we bring with us when we are born into incarnation on earth. You will remember, I said quite emphatically that the powers we bring with us from the world of the spirit are transformed into our inner organization. But any surplus created because the Christ impulse strengthens the impulse of the spirit does not have to be transformed during life on earth. For the evolution of the earth it will be necessary for more and more people to have the Christ impulse in the impulse of the spirit when they incarnate on earth. The spirit must grow stronger so that it is no longer active only until birth, when everything coming from the life of the spirit is transformed into inner organizing powers and we have only a small amount of conscious awareness to give us insight into our physical environment and what the brain-bound intellect is able to grasp. If human evolution towards the future does not mean that we gradually bring the excess of spirit with us that I have described, humanity will increasingly lose all feeling for the reality of the spirit. Earth life would then be wholly governed by Ahriman, a negative spirit, and people would know only the physical world they perceive with the senses, and what can be grasped with a brain-bound intellect. To some extent all this is developing now, at a time when humanity is in danger of losing the Holy Spirit.

It will not come to this, however. The science of the spirit is prepared to watch and see that humanity does not lose the spirit who comes to souls at the midnight hour and awakens the longing to see themselves and their true value in the past. The science of the spirit will have to speak more and more insistently of the Christ impulse, so that more and more of the spirit enters into physical existence through more and more people as they come to birth, and there will be growing numbers of people in physical existence who feel: Some powers in me must be transformed into organizing powers; but something dawns in my soul which does not have to be transformed. I am living in a body, but I have brought some of the spirit which belongs to the world of the spirit into the physical world. This will be the spirit which helps people to see what Theodora speaks of in my Mystery Play *The Portal of Initiation*: Human beings shall one day see the ether form of Christ.[4] The power of the spirit which thus enters into human bodies will become the eye of the spirit through which the worlds of the spirit can be seen and understood. People will first have to understand those worlds and then begin to see them, being able to understand. Vision will come because the spirit takes hold of human souls in such a way that they will bring this spirit into their physical bodies, and the spirit will shine even during incarnations on earth, first in a few individuals and then in a larger number. If we are able to say: The spirit, the Holy Spirit, wakes us up in the great midnight hour of existence, we must also say, considering the work the spirit is doing for the future evolution of earth: Even in the physical body, the best there is in human souls, the element that opens the worlds of the spirit for the inner eye, will be awakened more and more by the Holy Spirit as time goes on. Resurrected by the Holy Spirit in the midnight hour of existence, the human being will also be resurrected when he is in his physical body and coming to be at home in life on earth. Human beings will awaken inwardly as the spirit rouses them from the sleep which would otherwise envelop them so that they would see only the world of the senses and be able to use only the brain-bound intellect. This sleep would overcome humanity more and more, causing them to live in darkness, but the spirit will shine into it even on earth. In the midst of a life of mind and spirit which is dying because on the physical plane it has only the perception granted by the senses and by the world of the intellect, human souls will be resurrected by the Holy Spirit.

Per spiritum sanctum reviviscimus.

The St John's Building in Dornach

Short address given in Vienna before the lecture on 14 April 1914

BEFORE I START WITH TODAY'S LECTURE, I should like to say a few words, merely to let you know that this year we shall not be having the summer events held in the middle of summer in Munich in recent years. The next event of this kind is planned to be held in the St John's Building[1] and the building work is taking somewhat longer than originally planned. It is to be hoped that in the last two months of this year we shall reach the point where a festive opening ceremony can be held.

The building involves more work than you would normally expect and so you will no doubt understand that it has not been possible to have personal talks for a while.

I am sure there must be a number of reasons why it has not been easy for our Austrian friends to accept the idea that the St John's Building is so far away. Time does not permit me to go into detail but the truth is that karma led us to put the building where it is, and it will be good that we have done so.

It has to be acknowledged that we see this building as a kind of centre and symbol for our spiritual movement. Far away for some, it will be easy to reach for others — this is inevitable. It is to be hoped, nevertheless, that our Austrian friends will find ways and means of being present at this particular event in the St John's Building and that they will then experience this symbol of our anthroposophical movement to be their own — I want to say this expressly. In reality it is a symbol, not because of what it will be by way of a monumental building, but because if it really comes to be, this will only have been possible because some of our friends have been prepared to make extreme sacrifices in order that this difficult and, above all, expensive building project can be brought to completion in the form which it should have. The intention is to bring to expression what our spiritual movement is going to be. The whole style of the building has to be in accord with this. Everything which goes into the building project must be such that it is not in symbolic or allegorical form, but becomes part of the building in a truly artistic way. More than anything it has been necessary that for once there should be a building which, in all its forms, is the embodiment of the spiritual element which means so much to us. Different ages and civilizations have all had their characteristic buildings. The building which is to arise in Dornach will have forms that will provide a shell, or body, for our work in the spirit; and the way in which this shell comes together to enclose the inner and clothe the outer will bring something to expression which essentially has not been thought of before in architecture.

A Greek temple was built to be the dwelling place of a god; a Gothic cathedral to make a whole with the congregation gathered inside it. Our building is to be such that the forms immediately make it spiritually transparent. This means that when we are inside it, the architecture and the elements of sculpture into which the architecture continues on will give us the feeling: these walls do not merely shut off and enclose, which is what other walls have done until now; they are also communicators and will open the life of the mind and the spirit for infinite expanses of the spirit. They are walls which at the same time cancel themselves out because of their form and simply are not present in what they are in physical terms. What we hope to achieve is that everyone who is in the building and gradually comes to understand these forms – not as allegory or symbolism but through their own living inner response – will have a prospect open up into the world of which we are speaking, simply by entering into the form with a mind that is alive.

This is of course something new and unusual in architecture. It takes much time and work and, because of the way things are in our time — forgive me for putting it bluntly — it has needed and still needs money! Some of our friends have met our need with such a readiness to make sacrifices that we are able to say: this readiness to make sacrifices is in some respect also a sign of the way in which our spiritual movement has found understanding in human souls.

I wanted to say these words in the hope that you will take the building to your hearts and feel it to be like a focal point for our movement, so that you can feel united with it and grace it with your personal presence as often as can be in the future — once the building has been opened.

Notes

History of the German Text

Lectures of 6 April and 8 April 1914

In the earlier German editions, the text was based on the notes then available. Since then, more detailed notes taken by Georg Klenk of Munich have come to light. The text in the 5th German edition, on which this translation is based, has been based on these notes. On a few occasions, the original notes were more detailed and were used instead. Differences between the two sets of notes or mutually exclusive formulations are given below. Editorial additions to the German edition are given in square brackets.

Lectures given to members of the Anthroposophical Society on 9–14 April 1914. These six lectures lectures were probably originally written down by Rudolf Hahn or Reinach.

General Information
GA in references to literature refers to the German Rudolf Steiner Gesamtausgabe (Collected Works).

Lecture One   Public lecture given on 6 April 1914

1 Nicolas Copernicus (1473-1543). See Rudolf Steiner, *The Riddles of Philosophy*. Tr. F. Koelln. Anthroposophic Press, Spring Valley, New York 1973. Steiner also gave a lecture on Copernicus and his age in the light of anthroposophy on 15 February 1912 in Berlin (German text in GA 61).
2 The term 'natural science' is used where necessary to distinguish what is generally called 'science' today from the 'science of the spirit' (anthroposophy).

157

158   *The Inner Nature of Man*

3   The books were actually taken off the *Index* (of books Roman Catholics were not allowed to read) in 1757, but official permission to print was not granted by Rome until 1822.
4   The second set of lecture notes gives a slightly different phrasing: 'come in on the waves of the earlier life which was purely in the spirit and – please forgive the expression – clicks into place in the physical brain.'
5   It has not been possible to trace the exact phrase, but see *Faust*, Part 2, verse 4667: 'Begins to sound in ears of spirit/the new day now that has been born.' Goethe often spoke of the 'eyes of the spirit' or similar. Also in *Goethe's Naturwissenschaftliche Schriften*, volume 1 (GA 1a): 'We come to see with eyes of the spirit; without them we can only feel our way blindly in the study of nature as much as anywhere else.'
6   Instead of 'act in an entirely different way from the sum of powers', the second set of notes has: 'are entirely different from the sum of powers'.
7   Instead of 'You now live in the soul and spirit', the second set of notes reads: 'Your body is outside you.'
8   The second set of notes has 'philosophy' instead of 'physiology' here and in the sentences following.
9   Ernst Haeckel (1834-1919), German naturalist. Steiner frequently discussed Haeckel and his work, e.g. in *Rudolf Steiner, An Autobiography*, tr. by R. Stebbing (GA 28) Blauvelt, NY: Rudolf Steiner Publications 1977; and in a number of essays and lectures.
10 Wilhelm Ostwald (1853-1932), German chemist born in Riga, professor at Leipzig University and awarded the Nobel Prize in 1909. See R. Steiner's *Goethean Science* (GA 1), chapter 17: 'Goethe in Opposition to Atomism', tr. by W. Lindeman. Spring Valley: Mercury Press 1988.
11 'Life of the spirit' – the second set of notes reads: 'knowledge of the spirit'.
12 Jakob Fromer, 'Die Erneuerung der Philosophie', in *Die Zukunft*, vol. 21, No. 50, 13 September 1913. Not available in English.
13 Genesis 3: 5.
14 Goethe's *Faust*, Part 1, Auerbach's Tavern, line 2181-2. Tr. by Philip Wayne. Penguin.
15 Rudolf Steiner, 'Was soll die Geisteswissenschaft und wie wird sie von ihren Gegnern behandelt?' in *Philosophie und Anthroposophie*, Ges. Aufsétze (GA 35); in English as 'Spiritual Science: A Brief Review of its Aims and of the Attacks of its Opponents'. London: J.M. Watkins 1914.
16 Professor Laurenz Mueller (1848-1911), Inaugural Address, 8 November 1914: 'Die Bedeutung Galileis fr die Philosophie'; reprinted in *Anthroposophie* 1933/34, p. 29 ff. For Steiner on Mueller, see *Rudolf Steiner, An Autobiography*, Chapter 7, and Rudolf Steiner, *The World of the Senses and*

the *World of the Spirit*, lecture of 27 December 1911 (GA 134). Anthroposophic Press, New York 1979.
17 From Schiller's *Die Kénstler*, verse 12.
18 The second set of notes reads: 'how it stands face to face with the tempter in the present age.'
19 Baron Ernst von Feuchtersleben (1806-1849) *Zur Dietétik der Seele*, Vienna 1856, pp. 161-2 (Tagebuchblétter). The exact quote is, in translation: 'The human soul knows full well that in the final instance happiness can only be found by adding to its inner qualities and possessions.'

Lecture Two   Public lecture given on 8 April 1914

1 Gotthold Ephraim Lessing (1729-81), German writer and dramatist, in *Die Erziehung des Menschengeschlechts* (translates as: Educating the Human Race) 1780, 94: But why should it not be possible that every individual human being has been on this earth more than once?' and 95: 'Is the hypothesis so ridiculous because it is the oldest, because it was immediately apparent to the human mind before the sophistry of scholasticism dissipated and weakened it?
2 Henri Bergson, French philosopher. See his *Matiere et mémoire*, e.g. the following (translation of a passage from p. 254 of the German translation by W. Windelband, entitled *Materie und Gedéchtnis, Essays zur Beziehung zwischen Koerper und Geist*; Jena, 1908): It is now possible to see why memory could not arise from the condition of the brain. The condition of the brain makes a memory live on; it gives it power over the here and now by making it physical; but in its pure form a memory is something that is made known by the spirit. With memory, we have actually entered the realm of the spirit.
3 The second set of notes taken of the lecture has 'As we perceive', meaning 'As we see (it)', rather than 'When we perceive (with the senses)'. [The '(it)' has been added by the editors of the German edition.]
4 Rudolf Steiner, *The Threshold of the Spiritual World* (GA 17). Published together with *A Road to Self-Knowledge* (GA 16). Tr. by H. Collison. Rudolf Steiner Press, London 1990.
5 Rudolf Steiner, *The Soul's Awakening*, Scenes 5 and 6. In *The Four Mystery Plays*, tr. by Adam Bittleston. Rudolf Steiner Press, London 1983.
6 Instead of 'because they experience the consequences ... other earth lives', the other set of lecture notes says: 'because of what they do in consequence of having been born prematurely in one earth life'.
7 Incomplete sentence in the original. Translator.

8 Giordano Bruno (1548-1600), born in Italy; originally a Dominican, he began to doubt the dogma and went to Geneva but was driven out by the Calvinists. Later he lectured in Paris, but had to flee to London because of opposition from the Aristotelians. He also gave lectures at Oxford. After many more such moves he was taken prisoner by the officers of the Inquisition in Venice in 1592 and burnt in Rome seven years later. See his *De l'infinito universo e mondi. Dialogues about the infinite universe and the worlds.* In the third dialogue, Filotheo, the central figure among those involved in the dialogues, says the following, for instance:

I believe and maintain that beyond that imaginary vault of heaven there still is an ethereal region and in it an infinite number of cosmic bodies, stars, earths and suns, all perceptible in the absolute sense, both in themselves and for those who are on them or in their vicinity, although they cannot be perceived by us because of the distance.

9 Both sets of notes have 'unless they also understand life outside this *spiritual firmament*', because the word was probably misheard or the original notes misread. Another possibility, based on a German word that would have sounded similar, would be 'outside this firmament *of time*'.
10 The second set of notes has: 'that the true inner reality ...'
11 Johann Peter Eckermann, *Conversations with Goethe.* Conversation of 25 February 1824.

Lecture Three   9 April 1914

1 See also the lecture entitled *The Cosmic World and Individual Man*, given by Rudolf Steiner in Stuttgart on 2 May 1923. Published in *The Golden Blade* annual 1951.
2 Steiner R. *The Four Mystery Plays.* Tr. by A. Bittleston. Rudolf Steiner Press, London 1982.

> *The Soul's Probation*, scene 1 (pages 140-41):
> The spirit beings have implanted
> in human souls their labour's fruit.
> And he who lets the spirit seeds decay
> by his neglect, destroys the work of Gods.
> ...
> *(reading in a book the words of Benedictus)*
> 'Within thy thinking cosmic thoughts are living,
> within thy feeling cosmic forces weaving,

within thy willing cosmic beings working.
Lose thou thyself in cosmic thoughts,
experience thyself through cosmic forces,
create thyself from beings of will.
. . .
Thou findest aims of Gods,
knowing thyself in thee.

Lecture Four   10 April 1914

1   See note relating to lecture given on 8 April 1914.
2   *The Soul's Awakening*, Scene 6, pp. 445 ff.
3   Rudolf Steiner, *The Spiritual Guidance of Man and Humanity*. Tr. H. Collison, ed. H. B. Monges. 2nd edn. New York: Anthroposophic Press 1970.

'For we know that at birth man carries into the physical world what he has brought with him as the result of his former earthly lives. When he is born, his physical brain, for instance, is but a very imperfect instrument. The soul has to work a fine organization into that instrument, in order to make it the agent of everything that the soul is capable of performing. In point of fact, the human soul, before it is fully conscious, works upon the brain so as to make it an instrument for exercising all the abilities, aptitudes and qualities which appertain to the soul as the result of former earthly lives. This work on a man's own body is directed from points of view which are wiser than anything he can subsequently do for himself when in possession of full consciousness. (From Chapter 1).

Lecture Five   1 April 1914

1   Rudolf Steiner, *Secrets of the Threshold*. 4th lecture, Munich, 27 August 1913. Tr. by Ruth Pusch. New York: Anthroposophic Press 1987.
2   Earlier editions had 'following Ahriman', but in the current German edition this has been changed, for obvious reasons, to 'following Lucifer'.

Lecture Six   12 April 1914

1   Ludwig Laistner (1845-1896), a writer and specialist on mythology and literary consultant to Cotta's bookselling and publishing house in Stuttgart, Germany. He commissioned Rudolf Steiner to produce an edition of Schopenhauer's works and one of Jean Paul's. See *Rudolf Steiner, An*

Autobiography. The work he published was *Das Rétsel der Sphinx, Grundzége einer Mythengeschichte*, in two volumes. Berlin 1889.

2 Christoph Friedrich Oetinger (1702-1782), German theosophic theologian and pietist, a follower of Swedenborg. See his words: 'The physical body is the end of the works (often: 'the ways') of God,' in *Biblisches und emblematisches Wörterbuch* 1776, S. 407; see also Carl August Auberlen, *Die Theosophie Friedrich Christoph Ötingers nach ihren Grundzégen*, Tébingen 1847, pp. 446/7.

3 Rudolf Hermann Lotze (1817-1881), German idealist philosopher, professor of philosophy at Leipzig and Göttingen. As a physiologist, he fought the doctrine of vitalism. Rudolf Steiner is here referring to Lotze's *Grundzge der Religionsphilosophie, Diktate aus den Vorlesungen*, Leipzig 1894.

4 Georg Wilhelm Friedrich Hegel (1770-1831), one of the great German idealist philosophers, famous for his dialectical 'Logic', a system of logic, philosophy of nature and of mind. His philosophy is based on an underlying, all-embracing unity, the Absolute, which is a rational whole and is both true and real. See his *Vorlesungen ber die Philosophie der Geschichte* III, 3, 2. Kapitel: Das Christentum.

5 *Grundzége der Religionsphilosophie* (see 3 above), English title: *Outlines of a Philosophy of Religion*, London 1892, p. 172:

   We have shown reasons for believing that God is ever active in the world and upon individual spirits, and as we admittedly know nothing about the plan after which God governs the world, there is nothing in the way of our believing that at particular moments and in particular persons God has stood nearer to humanity and revealed himself more fully than in others.

   When, therefore, as a title of honour, the founder of our religion is called the Son of God, no serious objection can be raised; we are certainly justified in holding that the relation in which he stood to God was not only different in degree to that in which we stand, but also unique in kind.

   But no adequate expression can be found for what we mean in this case. In a literal sense Christ cannot possibly be the Son of God; it is a figurative expression and admits of no literal interpretation. There is, therefore, no room in this case for a theoretical dogma, and in affirming that Christ is the Son of God, we merely express our conviction of the unique importance which Christ has for us personally and his relation to God has for mankind; we cannot define either the one or the other.

6 Vladimir Soloviev (1853-1900), Russian philosopher. Works translated into English include *God, Man and the Church: The Spiritual Foundations of Life*, tr. by Attwater, J. Clarke & Co., London 1938; *Lectures on God-Manhood*,

Intro. by P.P. Zouboff, Dennis Dobson, London 1948; *War, Progress and the End of History: Including a Short Story of the Antichrist*, University Press, London 1915. See also *A Solovyov Anthology*, att. S.L. Frank, SCM Press, London 1950.

Important references by Rudolf Steiner are as follows: *From Jesus to Christ*, lecture of 7 Oct. 1911; *The Mission of Folk Souls*, lecture of 16 June 1910; *The Karma of Materialism*, lecture of 11 Sept. 1917; *Cosmosophy* vol. 1, lecture of 24 Sept. 1921; *The Human Soul in Relation to World Evolution*, lecture of 17 June 1922; Karmic Relationships: Esoteric Studies, lecture of 9 March 1924. (All published by Anthroposophic Press, New York, and/or Rudolf Steiner Press, London.)

Address   14 April 1914

1   The building with the double dome in Dornach, now generally referred to as the First Goetheanum, was initially to be called the St John's Building. It was not officially called the Goetheanum until 1918.

Lecture Eight   14 April 1914

1   Rudolf Steiner, *Theosophy: An Introduction to the Supersensible Knowledge of the World and the Destination of Man*, tr. by M. Cotterell, rev. A.P. Shepherd; London: Rudolf Steiner Press 1989. See the chapter entitled 'The Soul in the Soul World after Death'.
2   See, for example, Rudolf Steiner, *Manifestations of Karma*, lectures of 20 and 21 May 1910 in Hamburg, Rudolf Steiner Press, London 1984; *Karmic Relationships: Esoteric Studies*, vol. 2, lecture of 29 June 1924, tr/rev. Adams, Cotterell, Davy, Osmond, London: Rudolf Steiner Press 1974.
3   Rudolf Steiner, three essays (1905-6), now published in GA 34, *Lucifer-Gnosis*. English edition: *Anthroposophy and the Social Question*, tr. by E. Bowen-Wedgwood (out of print).
4   Rudolf Steiner, *The Portal of Initiation* (1910), tr. by A. Bittleston.

Steiner

A NOTE FROM RUDOLF STEINER PRESS

We are an independent publisher and registered charity (non-profit organisation) dedicated to making available the work of Rudolf Steiner in English translation. We care a great deal about the content of our books and have hundreds of titles available – as printed books, ebooks and in audio formats.

As a publisher devoted to anthroposophy...

- We continually commission translations of previously unpublished works by Rudolf Steiner and invest in re-translating, editing and improving our editions.

- We are committed to making anthroposophy available to all by publishing introductory books as well as contemporary research.

- Our new print editions and ebooks are carefully checked and proofread for accuracy, and converted into all formats for all platforms.

- Our translations are officially authorised by Rudolf Steiner's estate in Dornach, Switzerland, to whom we pay royalties on sales, thus assisting their critical work.

So, look out for Rudolf Steiner Press as a mark of quality and support us today by buying our books, or contact us should you wish to sponsor specific titles or to support the charity with a gift or legacy.

office@rudolfsteinerpress.com
Join our e-mailing list at www.rudolfsteinerpress.com

RUDOLF STEINER PRESS